A History of
Stanton
St Bernard

VAL KNOWLES

illustrations by
JACKY READ

First published in the United Kingdom in 2007 by The Hobnob Press,
PO Box 1838, East Knoyle, Salisbury SP3 6FA.

British Library Cataloguing in Publication Data
A catalogue record for this book is available from the British Library.

Picture Credits

The author and publisher are grateful to the following individuals and organisations for their kind permission to reproduce the maps, documents and artefacts listed below:

Dr Andrew Reynolds and Tempus Publishing for the map *Stanton St Bernard, Wiltshire — A late Anglo-Saxon Estate* reproduced from *Later Anglo-Saxon England, Life and Landscape*.

Wiltshire & Swindon Record Office and Wilton House for the Pembroke Estate maps of 1784 and 1853.

Wiltshire Record Society for the Andrews & Drury map of 1773.

Wiltshire Heritage Library, Devizes, for the catalogue of the 1917 Pembroke Estate sale, the watercolour of the church by John Buckler and the 'St Bernard Club' rulebook.

The Victoria & Albert Museum, London, for the image of the pincushion by William Fowle from the Calverley toilet set.

Wiltshire Heritage Museum, Devizes, for allowing the triquetra, the iron age pot and the palstave to be used as models for the line drawings.

The Downland Museum, Chichester, for the diagram of the watermill. The drawings illustrating Geffrey Burdon's inventory are based on 17th century furniture at the Downland Museum.

The Stanton St Bernard Millennium Committee and Rob Lindeman for the 'Millennium map'. Syd and Trish Woods for the Stanton Millennium photograph.

ISBN 978-0-946418-63-3

Typeset in 12/15 pt Joanna
Typesetting and origination by John Chandler
Printed in Great Britain by Salisbury Printing Company Ltd, Salisbury

*For the people of Stanton,
past, present and future*

Contents

The Village Name

T
HE VILLAGE NAME is intriguing. What St Bernard is doing in the Vale of Pewsey is a mystery. He seems to have slipped in uninvited but now lends distinction to the village.

Stanton is straight forward enough: it is 'stone tun' meaning stone town, settlement or farm and must derive from the many sarsen stones occurring on the lower land in the vale. In the Saxon charter of 903 the village is called simply Stantun. It is Stantone in the Domesday Book in 1086. Thereafter it is either Stanton or Staunton, the latter being frequently used in the 19th century.

As there are other 'stone towns' in the area, the name needed qualification. In the early Middle Ages, the village was sometimes known as Stanton Abbess, a reference to the landowner, the Abbess of Wilton. By the 16th century, Barnard or Bernard was being used. This is thought to refer either to the Berners family from whom Alton Barnes takes its name, or simply to the proximity of Stanton to Alton Barnes. There are some aberrations: Staunton FitzHerbard in 1402 and Stanton Fitzwarren in 1817 which is probably a simple mistake.

Stanton Barnard is used on maps dated 1787, 1791, 1792 and 1801. The map made in 1793 for the building of the Kennet & Avon canal gives the name as Stanton St Barnards.

St Bernard appears occasionally from the late 17th century. It was used more frequently from the late 18th century onwards, notably on Pembroke estate maps of 1784, 1847 and 1853, and was generally adopted from the mid 19th century.

Acknowledgements

THIS IS NOT the first history of Stanton St Bernard. I owe a debt to the late Naomi and David Corbyn whose book *Stanton and its people* was published privately in 1986, before the advantages of PCs and the Internet. I have drawn on their work and as this book progressed, my admiration for their research has grown even more.

The late Margaret Maxwell kindly gave me some valuable material and the advantage of her knowledge gained as an architect specialising in the care of historic buildings.

Thank you to the residents and ex-residents of Stanton for lending photographs, for the information and practical help so generously given and for making the preparation of this book so enjoyable. If I have omitted anyone, I apologise but appreciate your help nonetheless.

In particular I thank Jacky Read for her beautiful drawings; Melanie and Philip Humphries-Cuff for their enthusiastic help with the research and preparing the illustrations; John Chandler for his unrivalled expertise and patience and my husband Ray for his unfailing support - and for wielding his red pencil to good effect.

I am grateful to the following people for their professional advice and kind encouragement:

Eileen Bartlet
Sally and Lionel Beaven
Joan Brimacombe
Brian Crichlow
Vernon and Susan Faber
Chris and Del Fell
Mark Fell
John Fisher
Gillian and Michael Frankton

Ann Gimson
Joyce Hale
Bernard Lewis
Fred and Diane Nash
Charles Osborne
Vera Ostergaard
Frank Perry
Jean and Sonny Perry

Ken Player
Bryan Read
The late Jim Read
Edgar and Josephine Sainsbury
Rachel and Rob Schneider
Gerald and Wendy Tarver
Syd and Trish Woods
Peter Wyles

Professor John Barrett, Institute of Archaeology, University of Sheffield
Dr Lorna Haycock and Robert Moody, Wiltshire Heritage Library, Devizes
Dr Paul Robinson, Curator of the Wiltshire Heritage Museum, Devizes
Dr Andrew Reynolds, Institute of Archaeology, University College, London
The staff of the National Monuments Record Centre, Swindon
The staff of the Wiltshire and Swindon Record Office

1
Early People in the Vale

A s you approach Stanton St Bernard on the Pewsey to Devizes road, you can see on the hills evidence that people have been living in this landscape for thousands of years. Stanton is situated in the Vale of Pewsey. It is a long narrow parish running from the fertile valley floor up on to the chalk hills, the tip of its northern boundary pointing towards Avebury. To the south is Marden, site of possibly the largest henge[1] in Europe. The village of All Cannings is to the west, with the Neolithic enclosure of Rybury above it on Clifford's Hill. To the east are Alton Priors and Alton Barnes which has a Saxon church. The white horse carved on the hillside dates from the early 19th century. Dominating the skyline above the Altons is Adam's Grave, the long barrow set on Walkers Hill. The road north via the Altons to Lockeridge and Marlborough passes between Adam's Grave and the causewayed enclosure of Knap Hill with Golden Ball Hill further to the east. Amid all these archaeological riches, Stanton can claim six barrows and some ditches[2] but also a section of the mysterious Wansdyke which crosses the northern part of the parish.

However in the times before parish boundaries existed, the Vale of Pewsey was wetter and the hills were wooded. The flat valley floor was mostly marsh due to the springs emerging at the base of the chalk hills, forming streams which converge near Rushall to flow south to Salisbury Plain and join the River Avon.[3] It is thought that people mostly lived on the drier hills, venturing into the valley to hunt and fish, but the fragile evidence of early human activity is more likely to survive on the hills rather than in the valley where it can easily be obliterated by later settlement and centuries of agriculture. The availability on the chalk hills of the flint which is the raw material for tool-making attracted people to the area.

The earliest faint traces of people in the Vale date back to the Mesolithic period before 4000 BC. Hunting for wild pigs, deer and aurochs (wild cattle), they moved through the wooded countryside, seldom staying anywhere for more than a few days and leaving behind a scatter of flint implements, animal bones and the remains of their fire. Some sites were revisited from time to time and from the number of flint implements found there, Golden Ball Hill may have been a place which was regularly used.[4]

The early Neolithic peoples (4000 – 3000 BC) have left an imposing legacy. Theirs was a more settled existence. This is the period of the building of Adam's Grave, the West Kennet long barrow, Rybury and the causewayed enclosure of Knap Hill. No remains of domestic buildings have been found locally. However, from sites in other areas they appear to have been wooden structures with walls of daub and wattle measuring on average about 5 metres by 7.5 metres.[5] Small-scale farming by family groups was developing in clearings in the woods. The ard (a primitive plough) was introduced for land clearance. Cereals and pulses were grown, the diet being supplemented by gathering nuts and fruit. Animals were domesticated, cattle being especially important for meat, milk and skins.

The most durable remains of domestic life from this time are simple pots and the flint tools which were used for everything from cutting wood and hunting to preparing food and scraping the skins needed for many purposes, including clothing. Tools were evidently being made on Milk Hill, where flint occurs naturally. Finds include waste flakes and the cores of flints from which tools have been struck off, as well as scrapers and a leaf shaped arrowhead. A scraper with a semi-circular edge has been found near the dewpond, Oxna Mere.[6] Although there were undoubtedly specialist tool-makers with natural skills, it is likely that everyone, men and women, would have had to learn to make at least some of the tools they needed for everyday tasks.

The white chalk banks of the enclosures on Rybury and Knap Hill would have been a striking sight on the hilltops. The gaps in the ditches and banks, which do not seem to have had palisades on top, indicate that the enclosures were not primarily built for defence. Their exact purpose is not known. They were probably used as meeting places for the exchange of food, animals and goods and possibly to conduct ceremonies and for feasts. Excavations at the similar, but larger and slightly later, enclosure on Windmill Hill show that people lived there[7] but no conclusive evidence of occupation has been found at Rybury or Knap Hill. Not surprisingly, large numbers of worked flints have been found at both sites, together with sherds of pottery imported from more distant limestone areas.[8]

Adam's Grave still stands out today as a landmark on Walker's Hill to the west of Knap Hill, as its builders clearly intended. Its gleaming white chalk surface would have been an even more impressive sight in Neolithic times. Adam's Grave was excavated in 1868 by John Thurnam,[9] a pioneer in archaeology before scientific methods were applied to excavations. Thurnam was the Medical Superintendent of the Wiltshire County Asylum in Roundway Hospital, Devizes, who recognised the therapeutic benefits of physical activity in the open air and used his patients as an unpaid workforce on his digs.[10] He left the barrow disturbed and found the bones of several individuals and a leaf-shaped arrowhead.[11] Adam's Grave is thought to be similar in construction to the West Kennet Long Barrow which consists of several chambers built with large sarsen blocks and then covered with chalk rubble. At West Kennet, the chambers contained the bones of at least 46 individuals, deposited there over a period of perhaps 1000 years.[12]

By 3000 BC farming had been firmly established in the Vale of Pewsey and was to be the principal activity in the Vale for the next five thousand years. This was clearly not subsistence farming. The population was large enough and well enough nourished and organised to undertake cooperative building projects on a grand scale. The focal point of the community of farmers would have been the gathering place on Knap Hill, watched over by the dead in their imposing resting place in Adam's Grave.

During the next thousand years, developments were taking place further afield in which the inhabitants of the Vale must have been involved, working on construction or attending ceremonies. The grand ceremonial sites at Avebury and Stonehenge were constructed, with their stone circles and avenues. Silbury Hill was built. Henges were erected at Durrington Walls, Woodhenge and Marden. The henge at Marden which encloses 30 acres, is still marked by part of its bank and ditch, but it has been substantially damaged by farming activity, the two barrows within the henge being levelled in the early 19th century.

Stanton lies between two large henge monuments – Avebury in the north and Marden in the south, and is due south of Silbury Hill. Before the canal and the railway were built east-west across the parish and before the town of Devizes became prominent in the Middle Ages, the north-south route through Stanton must have been the most important. It is possible that a route between the two great henge sites was marked by large standing sarsen stones.[13] The Hanging Stone, with its Neolithic cup marks, still stands just over the parish boundary in Woodborough marking the site of a former ford. Travelling north, there was a standing stone near England's Bridge and another beside the road leading north

The Hanging Stone stands at the site of a former ford on the parish boundary with Woodborough and may have marked a prehistoric track.

out of the village opposite the church.[14] The Devil's Church Stone, broken up within the past 50 years, stood in the field below Milk Hill where the north-south path crosses the track to Tin Town.[15]

Prehistoric people were mobile and around 2400 BC new styles of weapons, tools and ornaments were appearing, the greatest innovation being the use of metal. These were associated with the Beaker people. This was the beginning of the Bronze Age. There was social change and the long barrows were no longer used for communal burials. An elite was emerging who buried their dead individually in barrows with their possessions. The richest graves, containing beautifully made weapons, tools and gold jewellery, are usually found close to the great ceremonial centres.[16] In Stanton the barrows on Harestone Down and on either side of Wansdyke on Milk Hill date from the Bronze Age. Sherds of Beaker and Bronze Age pottery have been found associated with these barrows.

The grave goods of the Beaker men reveal a lot about them. In addition to their bronze daggers and axes, flint arrowheads and polished stone wristguards, they also took to the afterlife their 'tool kits' for leather and metal working, small gold 'sun discs' and of course their beakers. These were quite large pottery drinking vessels, of distinctive shape and often elaborately decorated, which originally held alcoholic beverages, possibly mead.[17]

During the Bronze Age more woodland was cleared. People began to live a more settled existence on the high downland, on small farms with rectangular field systems and enclosures for stock, surrounded by ditches. A farmstead has been found on Bishops Cannings Down consisting of a roundhouse, 7 metres in diameter, and smaller buildings within an enclosure. Emmer wheat and barley were grown, milk, butter and cheese were produced and sheep, goats and pigs were kept. There is evidence of cloth weaving and leather working. Most of the tools used were flint; bronze was still a luxury. The farmstead was in use between 1200 and 1000 BC.[18]

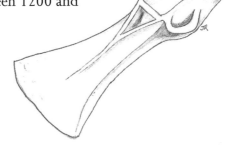

Bronze Age axe similar to the three damaged axes found in Stanton in the 19th century and now in the Salisbury Museum.

There was a late Bronze Age settlement on Golden Ball Hill and Knap Hill continued to be used. Some of the ditches on Milk Hill and Walkers Hill and on the high ground to the north are thought to date from this period. In Stanton three palstaves (a type of bronze axe) were found during the early 19th century and are now in the collection of Salisbury Museum.[19] Life was not all work in the Bronze Age: from a barrow in Wilsford, a flute made from the long bone of a swan has survived. Another – now lost – was found at Bishops Cannings.[20]

Around 900 BC there was a further technological development: iron began to replace bronze and made possible the production of more efficient tools and weapons. The late Bronze Age and early Iron Age was again a time of change and considerable expansion in agriculture. This transition period is still the subject of study.

A handle of a similar pot was found in Stanton. (Courtesy of Wiltshire Heritage Museum, Devizes)

In 1911/12 Maud Cunnington excavated an early Iron Age settlement of an unusual kind at Cannings Cross, to the west of Rybury. A large number of finds were discovered; jewellery and dress fittings such as pins and brooches, but in particular tools made of iron, bronze, bone and stone including equipment possibly for weaving. There was a great deal of pottery, some of a previously unknown type which is now named after the site. In addition, there was evidence of early iron working. The chalk floors of rectangular buildings were found and also post holes which could have been the bases of granaries or storage structures and a circular building. The site was probably occupied for about 300 years, with various phases of activity.[21] The handle of a pot, of the Cannings Cross type, has been found in the village of Stanton.[22]

In September 2003, a team from the University of Sheffield carried out an excavation at the Cannings Cross site. Aerial photographs showed areas of dark soil at Cannings Cross and also to the east of Clifford's Hill in Stanton. In 2004 the team excavated both these dark features which proved to be areas of waste material accumulated apparently for future use, perhaps as fertiliser. The soil contains a large number of pottery sherds and animal bones, predominantly cattle at Cannings Cross with more horses in Stanton. It is thought that the sites date to about 800 BC when people had just given up using bronze tools and were using iron from local sources. Preliminary analysis indicated that the area had been woodland and was cleared to enable the waste material to be deposited. So far features of this kind appear to be unique to this part of Wiltshire.[23]

The population increased during the Iron Age and the climate became cooler and wetter. The south of England was densely populated and the farms were larger than those of the Bronze Age. There is an Iron Age/Romano-British field system covering 170 acres on Harestone Down and Thorn Hill at the northern tip of the Stanton parish boundary. The 'Eald Burh settlement' south of Wansdyke, just outside the eastern parish boundary is thought to date from the Iron Age. A large number of Iron Age pottery sherds have been found on Milk Hill and a bronze brooch was discovered not far away. Brooches were not merely decorative at this time but were necessary to fasten clothing, as with modern kilt-pins.

As the population grew, due to immigration from Europe as well as by natural increase, distinct kingdoms emerged. The widespread re-use of neolithic enclosures as hillforts indicates that life was not entirely peaceful. Three main kingdoms are known in Wiltshire but there were also other, smaller groups. The extent of finds of their coins gives some indication of their areas of influence. It is likely that the Vale of Pewsey lay at the edge of the territory of the Dobunni, with the Atrebates to the east and the Durotriges to the south. Recently a distinct coinage with some similarities to that of the Dobunni has been identified in the Vale of Pewsey and the Marlborough area. It could possibly have been minted by another small tribe based at the major Iron Age settlement at Forest Hill, south-east of Marlborough.[24]

There had always been trade across the Channel and with the conquest of Gaul between 58 and 51 BC by the Romans, this trade intensified. Iron Age people were efficient farmers and there was a high degree of skill in metal work and cloth production. The Romans needed the metals, grain, wool, cloth and slaves available from Britain. The increasingly affluent British leaders began to aspire to the Roman lifestyle. High quality pottery, silverware, glass and jewellery were imported as well as foodstuffs and wine. The Wessex region is thought to have consumed more Italian wine than anywhere else in Britain at this time. The price could be high – there is a report that the cost of an amphora of wine (about 25 litres) could be one slave.[25]

When the Romans decided to add Britain to their Empire and invaded in 43 AD, not everyone here was unhappy. There was some armed resistance, and later the uprising led by Boudicca, but eventually a minority of fortunate Britons settled down to enjoy a higher standard of living in the new Roman towns and country villas.

There was a growing demand for food to sustain the new towns and the army, and for grain and wool for export to the empire. Cloth and finished garments were also exported. The birrus britannicus, a weather-resistant, hooded woollen cloak, was mentioned in an imperial edict on prices issued in AD 301. This must have been an essential purchase for Romans coming to Britain from the warmer parts of the Empire. A small stone carving exists showing each member of a family snugly enveloped in a birrus.[26]

For the farmers on Harestone Down daily work would have continued much as before. One of the main benefits of Roman rule to these farmers was the absence of tribal warfare. On the other hand, in their effort to increase agricultural production, Roman policy was to extend the amount of land under cultivation and incorporate the farms into estates centred on villas. A possible villa site has been identified at East Kennet which would be the nearest to the Harestone Down Farm[27]. This meant that the farms operated under management from the villa and that the farmers paid taxes. They would have had some access to the goods coming in from the Roman world. Pottery, brooches and coins dating from 1st to 4th centuries have been found on Harestone Down. They may have visited the small Roman town at Silbury Hill, or travelled along the new straight road eastward to the town of Cunetio (Mildenhall), or even westward to Bath. In the immediate neighbourhood there were settlements, or at least farms, at this time on Bishops Cannings Down and at Overton, Fyfield, East Kennet, Allington, Knap Hill and Honey Street.

From the third century AD the Roman Empire had been under increasing threat from internal dissension and attack by 'barbarians' (as the Romans saw

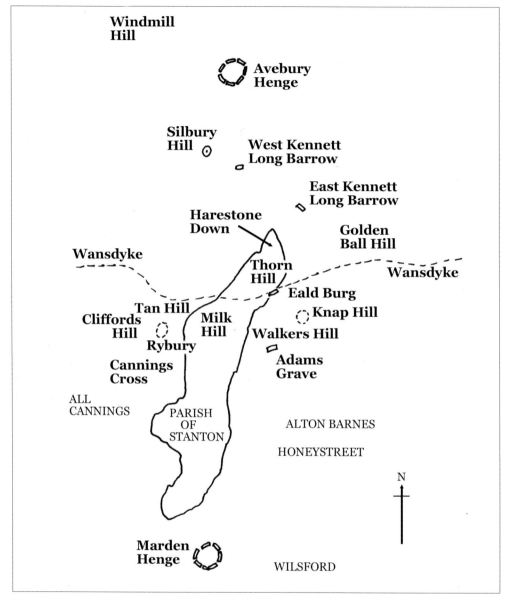

Sketch map of prehistoric sites near Stanton (not to scale)

them). As a frontier province, there had been unrest in Britain. New walls were built round Cunetio after 358 AD[28] and the first defences of the 'Saxon shore' against Saxon marauders based in Denmark had been constructed a hundred years earlier. In 407 AD the last Roman troops were withdrawn from Britain to fight on the Continent and Britain ceased to be part of the Roman Empire.

2

The Saxons
400–1000 AD

I T IS THOUGHT that life continued in the Roman towns and villas for some
time after the withdrawal of the Roman army, but there was no central
authority to maintain order. Someone buried his life savings – a pot containing
1200 gold, silver and bronze coins – at Stanchester near Wilcot in the early 5th
century and never came back to retrieve it.[29] This is just one small incident from
this chaotic and unpleasant time which has left a confusing archaeological record.

Local warlords appear to have emerged, some bringing in Saxon mercenaries
to bolster their power and help fight off invading Picts and Scots. Other Saxons
arrived as invaders and settlers. Excavation of a cemetery near Pewsey has shown
that a group of Saxons was living there from the mid 5th century, having come
from the Thames Valley area. The cemetery contains three graves of men, buried
with their weapons, who have been killed by battle injuries. This supports the
view that in the 5th and 6th centuries the Pewsey Vale was a battle zone in the
frontier area between the British and the incoming Saxons.[30]

The *Anglo Saxon Chronicle*[31] records a battle fought on Adam's Grave in 592 AD.
The *Chronicle* was begun by monks in the time of King Alfred in the 9th century.
Written so long after the event, the accuracy of the *Chronicle* cannot be totally relied
on but it is one of the few written sources for the period and however imperfect,
it gives an impression of this turbulent time. It states that by 519 a West Saxon
kingdom existed with Cerdic as its king. Over the next 70 years, Cerdic, his son

and his grandson Caewlin enlarged their territory by a series of battles against the Britons, at Salisbury, Barbury, the Isle of Wight and other unnamed places. When Caewlin became king he 'took many towns and countless spoils of war', including Gloucester, Cirencester and Bath. But in 592, the *Chronicle* records: 'There was great slaughter at Adam's Grave and Caewlin was driven out.' Bede, writing before 731, mentions that Caewlin, King of the West Saxons, was overlord of all the provinces south of the river Humber.[32]

Caewlin's successor was apparently unable to maintain this supremacy; Bede names King Ethelbert of Kent as the next overlord south of the Humber. In the early 7th century there were seven kingdoms, which were eventually consolidated into three: Wessex in the south, Mercia in the midlands and Northumbria in the northeast. Britain in the time of the Roman Empire had been nominally Christian, but the Saxons were pagans. Christianity gradually spread through the Anglo-Saxon kingdoms following St Augustine's arrival in Kent in 597, but this does not seem to have made them any less belligerent.

In 715 the hills north of Stanton were once again a battlefield when King Ine of Wessex fought King Ceolred of Mercia. Ine was a Christian king who had established his authority sufficiently to draw up a legal code and to try to govern his kingdom rather than acting merely as a warlord. Wessex at that time included Kent, Surrey and Sussex and was rivalling the powerful kingdom of Mercia. *The Anglo Saxon Chronicle* simply states that 'Ine and Ceolred fought at Adam's Grave'. No reason is given for the battle and the outcome is not recorded. It may have been an attempted invasion along the Ridgeway or a border dispute.

In a world without guns battles were a lot quieter though at close range the din was terrible. Anglo-Saxon soldiers fought on foot, forming the famous 'shieldwall' – a line of the strongest men standing shoulder to shoulder holding their shields in front of them with their spears thrust forward. The rest of the force stood behind, shooting arrows at the enemy and ready to fill gaps in the shieldwall as the injured fell. Once the shieldwall was breached,

Triquetra – Bronze ornament found in Stanton, now in the Wiltshire Heritage Museum, Devizes , used to decorate a hanging bowl or a horse harness. Thought to be either Iron Age or Saxon in date.

the battle became a brutal hand-to-hand brawl. Not every man could afford the protection of a helmet and chainmail. Horses were used only to bring supplies and the elite men to the battlefield and afterwards to pursue the enemy or to make a quick get-away.

As if this continual warfare between the English kingdoms were not enough the first recorded Viking raid on Wessex occurred in 789. Driven by the shortage of good farmland at home, the Scandinavians attacked the coastal regions of Europe and the British Isles. To 'go viking' meant to go raiding for plunder and slaves; later the objective was settlement. It was predominantly Danes who raided England and their invasions would continue for the next 300 years.

Uncooperative as they were, the English kingdoms managed to repulse Viking attacks for almost a century. Then the 'Great Army' of Vikings landed in East Anglia in 865 and successively defeated the English kingdoms. In 870 the Great Army attacked Wessex (now led by King Aethelraed and his brother Alfred) but met with strong resistance and withdrew to London. It was clear that the Great Army would return and neither Aethelraed nor Alfred underestimated the danger and magnitude of the task ahead. Alfred recalled later in his Will a meeting of the West Saxon Council held at Swanborough Tump in 871:

> But it came to pass that as we were all harassed with the heathen invasion then we discussed our children's future – how they would need some maintenance whatever might happen to us through these disasters. When we were assembled at Swanborough we agreed. . . that whichever of us survived the other was to give to the other's children the lands which we had ourselves acquired and the lands which King Aethelwulf gave us.[33]

Perhaps people from Stanton were present to hear this sombre discussion.

Alfred became King of Wessex that year after the death of his brother. Things did not go well. He suffered several defeats and was forced to buy the Vikings off. This gave him five years' respite which he used to reorganise his forces and was able to defeat a Viking attack in 877. But in January 878, the Vikings under Guthrum overran Wiltshire and Hampshire, mounted a surprise attack on Alfred's headquarters in Chippenham, and drove him back to Athelney in the Somerset marshes. The situation looked bleak, but Alfred rallied his supporters from Wiltshire, Hampshire and Somerset and in May defeated Guthrum decisively at Edington. Under the terms of the peace treaty, Guthrum became a Christian (Alfred stood as his Godfather) and agreed to withdraw with his army to East Anglia.

The Vikings now occupied the east and north of England – the Danelaw. Only the western part of Mercia and Wessex (which now included all of southern England) remained under English control. Knowing that the respite would be temporary, Alfred put Wessex on a total war footing. This policy was continued and developed by Alfred's son and grandson. For a time it contained the Viking incursions – though these could still be terribly destructive – and made possible the reconquest of the Danelaw in 919 by Alfred's grandson Edward and granddaughter Aethelflaed (who led the Mercians). In 920 Edward was chosen as overlord by the kings of the other smaller kingdoms and is known to history as King Edward the Elder. The heads of the royal house of Wessex were on their way to becoming kings of England.

The method Alfred used to achieve this success had a profound effect on the later social organisation of the south of England. The Vikings had the advantage of surprise. Their raiding parties remained in England until they had amassed sufficient booty and only then did they return to their ships and sail away. Alfred had the problem which always faced commanders of peasant armies fighting in their own country. After a while men began to worry about their farms, lost interest in the fighting, and went home. Alfred's solution was to mobilise half the rural men into the army, leaving the other half to look after the land so that food supplies were assured. In addition a network of 'burhs' or forts was developed which were garrisoned and supplied by the rural population. The burhs were a day's march from one another and provided an in-depth system of defence. Chisbury, Malmesbury and Wilton are local examples.

This continual warfare concentrated power and land in the king's hands. It led to the emergence of a military aristocracy of 'thegns' who came to form the elite of the standing army. The king granted estates to the thegns to ensure their loyalty and to enable them to equip themselves with weapons and armour and bring a body of armed men to the battlefield.

It is now time to look at the earliest surviving documents about the estate of Stanton St Bernard.

3

Charters, Boundaries and Wansdyke

I T IS NOT KNOWN how long the Harestone Down farm continued to be occupied after Roman rule ceased. The population decreased during this uncertain time due to unrest and a series of plagues, particularly a major outbreak in 530 AD. It is suggested that around 600 AD the watertable fell, making it possible to cultivate the lower land and build homesteads in the valley. Perhaps the successors to the Harestone Down farmers decided to move to lower ground where the houses would be hidden among the trees. Perhaps a group of Saxons came looking for land and settled. Archaeology does not yet provide an answer.

It is certain that farming communities were established in this part of the Vale of Pewsey by the early 9th century.[34] The charter for part of Alton Barnes dated 825, with its references to ploughlands, a sheepwash, lynches and a dairy farm, provides evidence for the type of farming in the Vale at that time.

The earliest surviving documents concerning Stanton are three charters dated 905,[35] 957 and 960. The first of these contains a reference to a grant of the estate by Aethelwulf (King Alfred's father) to his thegn Cenwold, who left the land to his son.[36] This grant must have been made between 837 and 858.

The charter dated 905 is a grant by King Edward the Elder (King Alfred's grandson) to 'Prince' Ordlaf, who was evidently going up in the world. In charters dated 900 and 901 he had exchanged land with the church to consolidate his holding in Lydiard Tregoze, and was described then as 'Count' Ordlaf.[37]

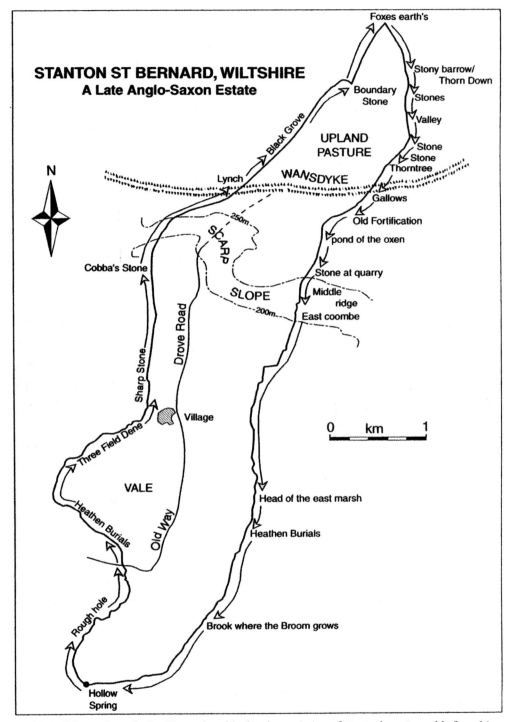

STANTON ST BERNARD, WILTSHIRE
A Late Anglo-Saxon Estate

Foxes earth's

Stony barrow/
Thorn Down

Stones

Valley

Boundary
Stone

UPLAND
PASTURE

Black Grove

Stone
Stone
Thorntree

Lynch

WANSDYKE

Gallows

Old Fortification

SCARP

250m

pond of the oxen

Cobba's Stone

Stone at quarry

SLOPE

Middle
ridge

200m

East coombe

Drove Road

Sharp Stone

Three Field Dene

Village

0   km   1

VALE

Heathen Burials

Old Way

Head of the east marsh

Heathen Burials

Rough hole

Brook where the Broom grows

Hollow
Spring

N

Map of Saxon boundaries (Reproduced by kind permission of Dr Andrew Reynolds from his book Later Anglo-Saxon England)

The charter of 957 is a grant by King Eadwig of '20 mansae (hides) at Stantune' to Oswulf, Bishop, 'free of all but the three common dues' (fortress and bridge work and military service). King Edgar confirmed this grant to Bishop Oswulf in the third charter dated 960.[38]

The grant to the bishop reflects the growing power of the church and the relative freedom from Viking raids at this time, although the usual obligations concerning defence and military service were imposed. Already, by the time of King Alfred's father, the kings of Wessex were granting land to the church and establishing monasteries, seeing the church as an ally against the heathen Vikings. Churchmen, being literate, played an important role as teachers, administrators and in the active diplomatic contacts with Europe maintained by King Alfred and his father.

The existence of two charters within three years is intriguing. The reason for this could lie in the short career of Eadwig who became king in 955 whilst still in his teens. He made an unfortunate start by failing to appear at the banquet which followed his coronation. With the assembled nobility becoming impatient, and hungry, the redoubtable Bishop Dunstan (later Saint Dunstan) went to look for Eadwig. He found the new king in his bedchamber making love to his girlfriend, the crown of England carelessly tossed on to the floor. At a time when kings maintained their authority by force of character and lavish hospitality to their supporters, this was indeed an insult to his entourage.

Eadwig died in 959, apparently not much regretted, and was succeeded by his brother Edgar. It is understandable that Bishop Oswulf would want to obtain confirmation of his land holding from the new king as soon as possible.

The next evidence for the tenure of Stanton is in the Domesday survey of 1086 when Stanton was held by the Abbey of Wilton but no charter relating to this survives. Bishop Oswulf is said to have 'lived and died' at Wilton so possibly it is through him that Stanton came to the Abbey.

The boundaries of the modern parish of Stanton St Bernard have altered little since the 10th century: they are essentially as set out in the charters, allowing for some minor differences between the three charters with regard to details of the bounds. This is the description given in the charter of 957:

> First to the Hollow Spring – to the Rough Hole – then to the Old Way – to the heathen burials – then to the three-field Dean – from the Dean to the Sharp Stone – then to Cobba's Stone – from the stone to a Row (of trees) – by a Lynch till it comes to Black Groves – then to the Boundary stone – from the stone to the Foxes'

Earths – then to the Stony Barrow on Thorn Down approaching it from the north – From the Barrow to the Stones along the Dean going downwards – from the Stone to a Stone – then to a Thorn-tree – then to the wrongdoers gallows on Wansdyke – then to the Old Fortification, meeting it on the middle of one side – from the Fortification to the Pond of the Oxen – then there lies a Stone at a Quarry – from the Stone to the Middle Ridge to East Combe – then to the Head of the East Marsh to the Heathen Burials – to the Brook where the Broom grows – then along the stream once more to the Hollow Spring.[39]

This sounds like the directions for a good walk. It is easy to imagine the king's representatives walking the bounds accompanied by two or three men from Stanton pointing out the landmarks, with a clerk in attendance making notes for the charter.

Most of the landmarks can be seen easily on the map and some are still visible on the ground today. A few terms may require explanation. The 'Old Way' is the road leading south from the village, curving towards All Cannings via Mill Farm. A dean (or dene) is a valley of a stream. A lynch (or lynchet) is a terrace formed by ploughing across a slope. The 'Stony Barrow' is still marked on the OS map as a tumulus. The 'Old Fortification' is the 'Eald Burgh' on the OS map, and of course the 'Pond of the Oxen' is Oxna Mere. The 'East Marsh' is at the boundary with modern Honey Street, so named because of the soft and sticky ground there.

The 'heathen burials' were probably the graves of criminals or other outcasts buried on boundaries rather than in the cemetery. In the case of suicides, this custom persisted at least into the 17th century.

The 'wrongdoers gallows on Wansdyke' was a gibbet, on which people found guilty of crimes were executed and their bodies left hanging to disintegrate. The Saxons often chose barrows or earthworks as execution sites, preferably on boundaries. The parish boundary of Stanton and East Kennet, on which the gibbet was sited, was also the boundary of the Hundreds of Swanborough and Selkley. This grisly landmark on the hill would have been even more visible on the skyline from the north than from Stanton. [40]

The hundred was an important Anglo-Saxon administrative unit covering, in theory, 100 hides of land, though some hundreds could be larger. The hide was the amount of land thought necessary to support a family, usually reckoned at 100-120 acres but the exact size varied according to the fertility of the land. The estate of Stanton contained 20 hides and was part of the Hundred of Swanborough.[41] The meeting place for the Swanborough Hundred was

Swanborough Tump, a barrow on the Woodborough to Pewsey road, marked now by a stone and a plaque.[42] Representatives from Stanton would undoubtedly have attended the hundred courts held regularly at the Tump to deal with administrative matters and law enforcement.

The boundaries of Stanton, like those of other villages in the Vale, enclose an almost self-sufficient farming estate, including upland pasture, arable, meadows, woodland and water sources. In doing this, the boundaries cross the Wansdyke and take in a considerable area of land to the north. This raises the question of the relative dates of the boundaries and of Wansdyke.

It is generally agreed that Wansdyke was built as a defence against a short-lived threat from the north, that parts of it are unfinished and that a large and well-organised workforce was needed to build it. Opinions on the date of construction of Wansdyke are divided. One theory, resulting from a study of the stretch of Wansdyke in West Woods, is that it was constructed in the late 5th century against the threat of a Saxon invasion and was based on the design of Hadrian's Wall with gates and towers at regular intervals.[43] Another view is that because our area was on the frontier between Wessex and Mercia in the 8th century and 9th centuries, Wansdyke could have been part of the defences of Wessex against the Mercians, who themselves had built Offa's Dyke on their border with Wales.[44] Certainly the social organisation necessary to build such a long defensive earthwork existed at that time.

It has been argued that such an impressive earthwork is an obvious feature to use to mark a boundary and the fact that the bounds of several parishes cross it indicates that they are older than Wansdyke. However if Wansdyke was constructed earlier, soon after the end of Roman rule, it would have lost its significance in the landscape by the time of the charters. The need for the estate boundaries to enclose sufficient land would override the convenience of using Wansdyke as a boundary. The fact that the Saxons ascribed it to their god Woden is put forward to support the view that Wansdyke was already ancient and mysterious by the time they arrived.

4

The Vikings Again

I F WE COULD go back in time and visit Stanton around the year 965, we would find rectangular wooden houses, roofed with thatch, laid out in an orderly pattern where the village is today. It is likely that each house and its outbuildings stood on its own plot, protected by a ditch and fence.[45] As the lord of the manor, Bishop Oswulf, lived at Wilton, there would have been no grand hall in the village. A church in Stanton is not mentioned until 1267 but it would be surprising if Bishop Oswulf did not make some arrangement for the spiritual care of his estate workers, even if it was only a cross in the open air where services were held. Alton Barnes still has its Saxon church and a church is mentioned in the charter of West Overton dated 972.[46]

The Saxons were tall, close to modern height. Women wore a long gown and a cloak, fastened on the shoulders with a pair of circular brooches. Personal items, including make-up brushes, combs and tweezers, were carried in leather bags suspended on their belts. Men wore knee length tunics, leggings and cloaks. Garments were made of woollen cloth, woven at home and, for more affluent people, dyed in bright colours. Everyone, including young children, carried a knife for eating and for use as a tool.[47]

England had been free from Viking raids since 954 after the reconquest of the Danelaw but in the 980s Danish attacks resumed all round the coast of England. The English king, Ethelred the 'Unred', although a competent ruler in peacetime, was not a decisive warrior as his forefathers had been. ('Unred' is traditionally translated as 'unready' but 'ill-advised' is more accurate, in all senses.)

In 991, when the Danes attacked Kent, Sussex and East Anglia, King Ethelred began the policy of buying them off with huge payments of silver.[48] Naturally the Danes came back for more and by 999 they were raiding the south coast from their camp on the Isle of Wight. These 'Danegelds' of between 22,000 lbs and 48,000 lbs of silver were paid repeatedly for the next 20 years. [49] The fact that these massive sums could be raised testifies to the potential wealth of England. Not surprisingly, the Danes eventually realised that rather than plundering such a rich country, it would be more profitable to conquer it.

For the people of Stanton, this meant paying high taxes to contribute to the Danegeld and to build the navy which the King failed to use effectively against the invaders. In 1008 the King decreed that each 310 hides was to provide one warship and each 8 hides a helmet and a coat of mail.[50] Worse than any taxation was the fear of a raid. In Stanton they must have heard reports of villages plundered and destroyed, the inhabitants killed or taken as slaves. It is thought that this happened to Collingbourne Ducis.[51] Year after year the devastation continued almost unchecked, largely due to incompetence and treachery on the part of English leaders. Some Stanton men must have been liable for military service in such a desperate time and may have seen some of the following events at first hand.

In 1003, Svein Forkbeard and his force landed in Devon. They attacked and destroyed Exeter which fell to them partly through treachery. *The Anglo-Saxon Chronicle* tells the sorry story of what happened next:

> A very great army was gathered from Wiltshire and Hampshire, and went very resolutely against the force. The earldorman Aelfric should have led the army, but he displayed his old wiles. As soon as they were close enough to one another, he feigned sickness, and began retching to vomit, and said that he was taken ill; so he betrayed the people he should have led, as it is said: 'When the war-leader weakens, all the army is greatly hindered.' When Svein saw that they were not resolute, and all scattering, he led his force into Wilton, ravaged and burnt the borough, went to Salisbury, and from there went back to the sea, where he knew his wave-coursers were.

There was a famine in England in 1005 and the Danes stayed away. The following year a battle was fought at East Kennet. Svein Forkbeard's force was returning along the Ridgeway to its base on the Isle of Wight, having rampaged through Hampshire, Berkshire and Oxfordshire, looting and burning as it went. An army of Wiltshire men had gathered at East Kennet to make a stand against the

Danish force.[52] The Chronicle reports, 'Soon that army was put to flight, and afterwards the people of Winchester could see the force proud and unafraid, that went by their gates to the sea'.

In 1010, the Danes again came perilously close to Stanton. A large Danish army under Thorkell the Tall had landed in Sandwich in 1009 and for the next three years terrorised southern England and East Anglia. Having burned Northampton, Thorkell decided to invade Wessex. He got as far as Bishops Cannings, which he burned. He was stopped at 'Cannings marsh' and returned towards the east. Presumably this was marshy ground near All Cannings, but the information available is frustratingly scant.[53] What damage the Danes may have done in the villages of the vale is unrecorded.

The English government was by then in disarray. The Chronicle, always critical, is scathing: 'The counsellors were all summoned and it was discussed how this land should be defended, but whatever was counselled then, it did not last longer than a month. Next, there was no head man who would gather the troops, but each fled as best he might; furthermore, no shire would help the other next to it.'

Svein Forkbeard's objective now was to become king of England. Knowing that many people were longing for effective government, he returned to England in 1013 and was accepted as king. Ethelred fled to France. Svein's sudden death five weeks later led to a struggle for the crown. Finally, in 1016 Svein's son Cnut (or Canute) became King of England, proving to be a capable ruler who ensured almost twenty years of much-needed peace.

Stanton now belonged to the Abbey of Wilton, a religious house for women where girls from noble families could receive an education. The Abbey had always been generously supported by kings and by ladies of the royal house. The first prioress was the sister of King Egbert and many royal women were educated at the Abbey or became nuns there. The Abbey could be described as the most prestigious girls' 'finishing school' of its day.[54]

Sometime in the 960s, King Edgar visited Wilton Abbey and fell in love with Wulfthryth, a nobleman's daughter, who was being educated there. Their liaison resulted in the birth of a daughter, Edith, born in Kent. Edgar was of course already married and Wulfthryth returned to Wilton Abbey with Edith and took the veil. This seems to have been a genuine love affair on King Edgar's part because when his wife died some years later, he asked Wulfthryth to marry him. By this time she had become the Abbess and she turned him down. Edith spent her entire life at Wilton Abbey, acquiring such a reputation for piety that she was canonised after her death in 984 at the age of 23. Miracles were reputed to have occurred at her tomb at Wilton, attracting many pilgrims who added to the prosperity of the Abbey. King Canute is said to have built a shrine to St Edith at Wilton and to have paid for the repair of the church there.

With its royal connections and the popular cult of St Edith, Wilton Abbey survived the upheaval in land holdings which followed the Norman Conquest. William of Normandy, though greedy and ruthless, was a pious man and generally allowed the great religious houses to keep their land, whilst the Saxon landlords were everywhere replaced by his Norman henchmen. Thus the people of Stanton experienced no change of landlord after the great events of 1066.

5
The Wilton Abbey Estate

TWENTY YEARS after he became king, William and his court were in Gloucester in midwinter.

'The King had great deliberations and very deep speech with his counsellors about this land, how it was occupied and by what men. He then sent his men all over England into each shire . . .and he let it be written down . . .what and how much each man was holding in land, in livestock, and how much money it was worth. . .and all the documents were brought to him afterwards.[55]

The survey, which we know as the Domesday Book, was completed in twelve months. It had two main uses: for taxation and as an official register of land holdings after the many changes which had taken place since 1066.[56]

The entry for Stanton gives the first glimpse of the people working here and reads:

The Church of St Mary of Wilton holds STANTONE. Before 1066 it paid tax for 20 hides. Land for 12 ploughs. Of this land 10 hides in lordship; 4 ploughs there, 8 slaves there. 16 villagers, 1 smallholder and 21 cottagers with 8 ploughs. 2 mills which pay 12s. 6d; meadow, 60 acres; aldergrove, 3 acres; pasture 1 league long and ½ league wide.[57] The value was £16; now £24.[58]

The first figure of £16 is the valuation before 1066; the second (£24)

TERRA ÆCCLÆ WILTVNIENSIS.

.XIII. ECCLA S MARIE WILTVNIENSIS teñ STANTONE.

T.R.E.geldb p.xx.hiđ.Tra.ē.xii.caī.De hac tra

st in dñio.x.hidæ.7 ibi.iiii.caī.7 ibi.viii.ferui.Ibi

xvi.uilti 7 uñ borđ.7 xxi.cofcez.cũ.viii.caī.

Ibi.ii.molini redđ.xii.fot 7 vi.deñ.7 lx.ac pti.7 iii.ac

alneti.Paftura.i.leu lg.7 dimiđ leu laī.

Valuit.xvi.lib.Modo.xxiiii.lib.

Facsimile of entry for Stanton in the first printed edition of Domesday book.

represents the value in money rents or goods which the Abbey might expect from its holding and is of course the basis for taxation.

A hide[59] is reckoned at 100 to 120 acres, as we have seen, giving a total area of approximately 2000 – 2400 acres. Of this, half was 'in lordship', that is to say, it was being farmed directly for the benefit of the Abbey. This was known later as the demesne farm. The remainder of the estate was divided among the estate workers listed.

Stanton was unusual in having two mills, obviously thanks to an abundant water supply. Most other villages of similar size in the Vale had one mill each. Alton Priors, Echilhampton, East Overton, Beechingstoke, Draycot Fitzpaine and Wilcot had no mills. Wilcot however had other compensations. The surveyor, usually parsimonious with adjectives, became positively mellow in Wilcot which had a 'new' church, a 'very good' house and a 'good' vineyard.

The presence of slaves owned by a religious house is a shock to modern minds. The Saxons had always been a slave-owning society, but attitudes were already changing prior to the Conquest and there are instances of landlords granting freedom to their slaves in their wills as acts of piety. People became slaves by being captured in battle, through economic misfortune, as a punishment for crime or being born to parents who were themselves slaves. The slaves are usually listed with the ploughs in Domesday and so are thought to have been mainly employed as ploughmen. Slavery died out during the following 50 years, some slaves buying their freedom and others being settled on small plots of land.

The other people mentioned were also 'unfree' in the sense that they could not move away without their lord's permission. They held their land in return for working for specified periods on the lord's farm, which could be extremely irksome at times when their own holdings required attention. There were local and regional variations in the size of the holdings and in the obligations due to the lord.

The 16 villagers (or villeins) were the highest class of peasants who might each farm 30 or more acres of land in the common fields. Below them came smallholders who held less land than the villagers but more than the cottagers, probably around 10 acres. The 21 cottagers each had a small house and a plot of up to 4 or 5 acres of land. The Domesday survey lists only the land-holders and the slaves who worked on the land: a total of 46 people. To obtain an estimate of the population of the village, it is usual to multiply this figure by four to five, which works out at between 184 and 230 people. There must also have been a number of landless men working for the Abbey's farm and for the villagers who farmed the larger areas of land. The blacksmiths, carpenters, shepherds and other specialists vital to village life were doubtless to be found among the cottagers or landless men.

Stanton of course had been a valuable estate for at least the past 200 years. It is thought that the system of farming which lasted into the 18th century was already practised at this time. The low-lying arable land was divided into large fields, which in turn were sub-divided into strips and allocated to individual tenants. In this way, everyone had a share of the good and of the less fertile land. The large fields were worked in rotation and allowed to lie fallow in alternate years to keep the soil in good heart. The map produced in 1784 for the purpose of abolishing the strip system, gives an idea of its complexity. Naturally, the area under cultivation was smaller at the time of Domesday and varied down the centuries according to population size and economic conditions.

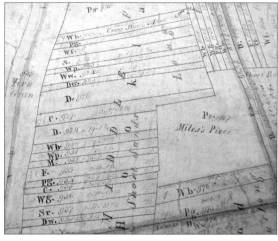

Detail of 'strips' from 1784 Pembroke Estate map

Sheep were a key element in this system. Most tenants had the right to keep a certain number which were pastured on the hills in common flocks and brought down on to the arable fields at night to manure the land prior to sowing or whilst it was lying fallow. The village flocks were in the care of shepherds who were responsible for lambing and for erecting 'folds' – temporary enclosures made from hurdles which confined the sheep to the areas on which they were to graze. In addition to their primary role of maintaining the fertility of the arable land, the sheep provided meat and wool, initially for domestic cloth production, and later for the growing Wiltshire cloth industry.

The meadow land, mostly in the wetter southern area, provided grazing for cattle. Also in the south were the 'aldergroves'. The alder prefers a wetter environment and often grows along streams. The woodland would have been carefully managed as the village depended on it for fuel, raw materials for hurdles, tools, baskets and furniture and for building construction. Pigs were often allowed to forage in woodland.

The two mills were located on or very near the sites of the present Mill Farm House and Stanton Dairy. The mill machinery would have been made of wood; oak or elm for the waterwheel and shafts and elm for the internal gear wheels, with some metal banding on the shafts for reinforcement. Watermills were known from Roman times and in the earliest types the wheel was turned by the natural force of the stream. Later, streams were dammed to create a millpond so that the flow of water could be regulated. The millponds naturally became a useful source of freshwater fish. Millers were often paid by retaining some of the corn brought to the mill to be ground and in turn paid rent to the lord. Presumably the two Stanton mills also served other villages which had no mills.

Twelve ploughs are mentioned at Stanton in the Domesday survey: 4 on the abbey farm and 8 shared by the tenants. The heavy wheeled plough with its iron blade was pulled by a team of 8 oxen and required two men, one to guide the plough and the other to direct the oxen with a long goad or rod. (The length of this rod is the origin of the measurement in 'rod, pole or perch'). The oxen were powerful but the team was cumbersome to turn, hence the shape of the long, narrow strips of land allocated to the tenants. Later in the Middle Ages horses were introduced for ploughing, as they were quicker and more manoeuvrable than the oxen.

This system of farming required a high degree of regulation and cooperation. Which fields would lie fallow, which crops would be grown on the strips in each field, when and where the sheep would be folded on the land, the use of the communal ploughs, all this had to be decided and the decisions respected by everyone. To achieve this, manor courts, 'courts baron', were held in the village every three weeks. The abbey or demesne farm was managed by a steward or reeve who naturally presided over the court which the tenants were obliged to attend. Here the decisions were made and communicated, disputes were settled and action taken against transgressors. A body of knowledge was built up known as the 'customs of the manor', which set out the broad agricultural routine for the year, rights of access, and rights concerning the transmission of tenancies.

Although there was no 'lord' residing in Stanton, it is likely that the Abbey's steward enjoyed a large and comfortable house, surrounded by the demesne lands or 'inlands'. ('Inlands' became a field name and later was corrupted to 'Englands' as in Englands Bridge over the canal today.) It is now thought that, contrary to former belief, all peasants at this time did not live in hovels along with their livestock. Few examples of houses of this period remain standing today, but from excavations it appears that the more prosperous villagers had well built timber framed houses, often of cruck construction and cob walls, standing in their own plots with barns, pig sties and outbuildings for the animals. Cooking would be done on an open hearth in the middle of the room, with the smoke escaping through the roof. Some houses had bread ovens. The cottages were more modest, mostly consisting of one or two cramped rooms. Windows were small and unglazed; wooden shutters kept out the wind. People had little furniture but the local carpenter could meet his customers' few needs throughout their lives: he made the crib for the new baby, beds, tables, benches and finally, the coffin.

The Abbess of Wilton, in common with the heads of the other important nunneries of Winchester, Barking and Shaftesbury, was a baroness of the realm by virtue of her office and on at least one occasion, in 1306, the Abbess was summoned to attend Parliament. She held her lands from the king, one of her obligations being to provide five knights to serve with the king's army. The Abbess sent knights on the king's expedition to Wales in 1223, to Bedford the following year, and four times between 1277 and 1327.

To raise this money, the Abbess made grants of land 'for a knight's fee' or 'scutage'. In 1166 eight such tenancies were in existence; one was a holding of two hides in Stanton by Walter of Calstone who was jointly responsible with Gerard Giffard for the cost of one knight. A document exists (dated between c 1220-40) granting this land in Stanton by Philip of Calstone to his grandson Robert Burdon for a knight's fee. The Burdon family would be prominent in Stanton for the next four hundred years.

Tenants holding land for a knight's fee were required to attend the court of the Belhouse in Wilton. The Abbey also had a tradition of entertaining its principal tenants to a meal on 26th December, the feast of St Stephen. This would have meant a cold ride across Salisbury Plain, a journey also regularly made by the Abbey's officials overseeing the estates in Stanton, Overton and North Newnton and by pack horses and carts laden with produce for the Abbey.

During the 12th and 13th centuries there were generally good harvests and population growth. Presumably the people of Stanton shared in this prosperity but it is likely that the village was being put under pressure during the 13th century by Wilton Abbey which was getting into financial difficulties in spite of its rich endowments. In 1229 royal letters were issued requesting tenants to contribute to the relief of the abbey. The cathedral at Old Sarum was moved to Salisbury in the mid 13th century and the main road to the west of England was diverted to run through Salisbury instead of through Wilton. This diminished the trade and importance of the town of Wilton and the Abbey's revenues fell as a result. One way in which landlords at this time were exacting more money from their tenants was through the manor courts, raising the 'fines' payable on marriage or on a change of tenancy. For example, in Stanton in 1293 Robert Turbun paid 33s 4d to the manor for the right to take over the land holding of John Hughes and marry his widow, Alice.[60]

In 1246 the abbey buildings were in very poor condition and although the abbess received a grant of oak trees from the king for repairs, she was in trouble that year for 'assarting' or clearing woods on her holding in Savernake Forest without permission. Discipline was lax at the abbey and spending was high. From a fragment of a kitchen account book covering 17 weeks which survives from this period, it appears that it cost between 10 shillings and £1 per week to feed the nuns. There are also details of a great feast to celebrate the installation of a new abbess, when the delicacies included swans, peacocks and venison plus 60 gallons of milk.

It is highly unlikely that such opulent fare was available in Stanton. In fact the next reference to an individual in Stanton at this time is a sad one. It is in the record of the king's justices in the shire court in 1249:

Isabel, who was the wife of Simon German, was found dead in her bed in Stanton. The first finder does not come, having died. No one is suspected. Judgement:

misadventure. The townships of Wodelstok, Stanton and Aulton Priors did not come to the inquest. So they are in mercy.[61]

Font – thought to date from the 12th century.

Being 'in mercy' means being subject to a fine at the court's discretion. As the king's justices only visited a neighbourhood about once every 7 years, it is perhaps not surprising that no local people attended the inquest. However imperfect this system was, at least it brought the king's justice to ordinary people who previously only had recourse to the manor courts which were dominated by the landowners.

The first mention of a church in Stanton occurs in 1267 although a church was almost certainly there before that. The existing font is thought to date from a century earlier. The revenue of Stanton church from the glebe land was used to support a prebend at Wilton. The prebendary, the holder of this office, was attached to the abbey church. His original duties included saying mass for the nuns and assisting with the administration of the abbey. The prebendary had a house in Wilton and in theory paid a vicar to look after the congregation in Stanton.

The saints' days and the great church festivals of Christmas and Easter punctuated the year and were occasions for celebration and relaxation. Echoes of the old pagan festivals remained. Thanksgiving for the harvest had a very personal significance lost to us today. People in the Middle Ages knew only too well that they faced hunger, disease and very possibly death if the harvest failed. The church was the most impressive building in the village. Its colour, light and music could be experienced by everyone although the Latin of the services was a barrier to full understanding and participation by the congregation. The price paid for the church by the people was the tithe, one tenth of the produce of the village.

The business of the village was marked by the church's calendar. 1st January was not 'New Year's Day' until 1752 when the Gregorian calendar was adopted. Before that the year began on 25th March: 'Lady Day', the feast of the annunciation of the Virgin Mary. This was the first of the quarter days on which rent was due and tenancies began and ended. Then came Midsummer 24th June, Michaelmas 29th September and Christmas 25th December. Candlemas 2nd February, Lammas 1st August and Martinmas 11th November were other significant days in the agricultural year. Other dates were usually expressed in terms of the nearest saint's day.

6

Taxes, Plagues, and the End of the Abbey

P OOR HARVESTS in the 1290s presaged a long period of hardship. A series of failed harvests began in 1314, caused by unusual climatic conditions. There was disease among the sheep and cattle. The famine in the years 1314 to 1322 is thought to be the most severe ever recorded in England. The price of wheat rose to 16 shillings per quarter from its usual price of 5 or 6 shillings. People tried to sell their draught animals to buy food, but the price fell because no one could afford them. The death rate rose and the courts were full of accusations of thefts of food.[62] Stanton people must have suffered like everyone else, depending totally as they did on the harvest and their animals.

There is little good that can be said of tax-gatherers but they do provide information for the historian. The next we hear about at least the better-off people in Stanton comes from a taxation list of 1332. Parliament had granted Edward III a fifteenth and a tenth of the movable goods of the laity of the realm. The 'fifteenth' applied to country people and the 'movables' subject to tax were farm livestock and agricultural produce but not agricultural implements, household goods and food not for sale. People with taxable assets valued at less than ten shillings were exempt. Assessors – 134 of them for Wiltshire – were appointed. The people eligible in Stanton, and the amount of tax they had to pay, is as follows:

John Burdoun	5s 2d
Nicholas Selewyne	3s
William Stour	2s
Richard Cocke	4s
John Scot	2s
Johyn Mayde	4s
Adam Maynot	1s 8d
Robert Giffarde	2s 6d
William Edmond	8d
Robert le Reve	4s 4d
John att Stoniefforde	3s 4d
Peter Rolfe	4s
Thomas Turbone	4s

Fire surround from Laburnum Cottage –
survival from a grand house, now disappeared.

These 13 people were liable to pay a total of 40s 8d. in tax. This compares with 10 people in Alton Barnes (38s 4d), 10 in Marden (33s ½ d including 'Isabel, the king's mother 6s 8½ d'), 10 in Woodborough (27s 4d), 10 in Oare (41s 5¾d) and 14 in Wilcot (34s 10d).[63]

John att Stoniefforde is clearly the miller at Stoniford Mill which was on the site of the present-day Mill Farm. Robert le Reve is identified by his office, and was presumably in charge of the demesne farm.

There had been sporadic wars with France and the Scots for the past 50 years, but in 1337 Edward III claimed the throne of France and the Hundred Years' War began. Taxes continued to be regularly demanded, but now they were based less on personal assessment and more on agreement between the assessors and local representatives.

In 1348 bubonic plague reached England, borne by fleas on rats from a ship which docked in Weymouth in Dorset. It is estimated that the Black Death killed between one third and one half of the population in two years. The social consequences were immense throughout the country. Whole families could be wiped out or severely depleted and houses and land holdings left empty. The survivors had the opportunity to acquire more land but would not necessarily need the houses. Abandoned plots and ruined buildings were a feature of the countryside for many years to come.

Because of the labour shortage craftsmen and agricultural workers demanded higher wages. Many unskilled men took the opportunity to enter skilled occupations. In the villages landlords struggled to maintain their customary rights over the lives of their remaining tenants. The latter were more prepared to leave and start new lives elsewhere free of feudal obligations, often preferring short-term contracts or casual work which gave them greater freedom. Women's property rights were improved: they could hold joint tenancies with their husbands which enabled them to retain their land holding if they were widowed. The government responded by passing legislation[64] limiting wages to the rates prevailing before the Black Death, penalising workers who broke their contracts and imposing restrictions on beggars and on people travelling in search of work.[65] These measures were unpopular and widely flouted. However, when a return was made for Wiltshire concerning wage levels, Stanton was found to have no one 'in excess'.[66]

In spite of the horror of the Black Death and the consequent social upheaval, the economic life of the country continued. There was no reduction in wool exports[67] during the time of the Black Death and Wiltshire was not excused payment of the tax of 'Fifteenths' unlike some of the other counties where the plague had had a devastating effect. Mortality was very high in Salisbury but knowledge of the death rate in the villages is patchy and nothing is known of the situation in Stanton. There were further sporadic outbreaks of plague and other epidemics during the rest of the century and the population of England did not return to its pre-Black Death level until Tudor times.

The French wars continued and taxation was heavy, taken from a smaller population of taxpayers. People were suspicious of government corruption and incompetence. In 1377 a 'poll tax' of 4d per head was imposed on everyone over the age of 14 who was not classified as a beggar. This was judged unfair as it weighed most heavily on low wage earners. In Stanton, there were 76 people liable to pay.[68] The threat of further taxation of this kind brought discontent to a head in 1381 with the Peasant's Revolt in East Anglia and the South East. Although the revolt was put down, it made both government and people aware of the power of a well-organised popular movement.

The situation at Wilton Abbey again gave the ecclesiastical authorities cause for concern. In 1379 the Bishop of Salisbury investigated and imposed measures to put the administration on a more business-like footing, less open to abuse. The abbess was ordered to supervise the infirmary regularly and to eat the same food as the nuns (previously special bread and ale had been prepared for her exclusive use). The nuns were told to reprove their pupils kindly and were forbidden to indulge in superstitious games or plays. The enclosure rules limiting the nuns' contact with the outside world were to be more strictly enforced.

By 1423, the affairs of the abbey were reported to be in better order. Being under royal protection, the abbey was often obliged to provide maintenance or pensions for the king's nominees, for example in 1347 paying a pension of £5 a year for one of the king's clerks until a suitable benefice could be found for him. The prebends of Chalke, North Newnton, South Newton and Stanton gave the abbey valuable opportunities for patronage but also made it subject to political interference.

The list of vicars of Stanton whose names are known begins with William Palmere in 1362. The church is thought to have been built in the 14th century in a simple version of the early Perpendicular style. This style was developed after the Black Death when there were few masons. The stone was dressed at the quarry, possibly in the Corsham area, and brought to the site.[69] There is a record that new windows were put into the north wall of the nave and chancel of the church in the 14th century.[70] The first illustration of the church, a tiny sketch in the margin of the Pembroke survey dated 1567, shows a low rustic building attached to the imposing and slightly incongruous tower (which still stands), built a century later than the church. The next illustration is a watercolour by J. Buckler painted in 1807 showing apparently the same building, the thatched roof of the church having been replaced by lead.

Residents of Stanton next make their appearance in the record of a court held on 14th April 1439 at Swanburgh, probably at or close to Swanborough Tump. This was at the Sheriff Turn when the Sheriff or shire reeve periodically made a circuit of the county holding courts to try the cases brought to him by the tithingmen of each locality, who were responsible for keeping the peace. Edward Brid and John Gye, millers of Stanton, were fined for an unspecified offence (possibly giving short weight). John Jakys was ordered to clear out his ditches because the highway was under water – a situation all too familiar today.[71] A glimpse of fifteenth century life is seen from the following passage:[72]

In the seventeenth year of the reign of Edward IV (1477) Thomas Clyff of Staunton near Devizes, chaplain, in the dawn of the Sunday next before the feast of St Mary Magdalen, armed with a sword and a bow and arrows broke open the door of the church of All Saints at Staunton and carried away an ivory pyx[73] bound with silver worth 13s 4d, two garments of lawn worth 3s 4d and 25 pounds of lead to the value of 16d in the custody of the church wardens, and that the same chaplain on the night of Monday September 8th in the sixteenth year (1476), armed with a sword and stick broke into the close of John Bonde at Staunton and stole 10 capons worth 8d each and 60 cocks worth 7d each and 20 ducks worth 3d each.

The church appears to have been well, if not richly, equipped. The reference to John Bonde's establishment gives a village picture of houses and gardens enclosed presumably by thatched cob walls.'[74] Thomas Clyff, who had been vicar since 1472, not surprisingly left Stanton in 1477.

During the early part of the 16th century, new ideas on religion were in the air. People wanted to read the Bible and to hear church services in English. The established Catholic church was seen as corrupt and too rich, providing jobs for the indolent at the expense of working people. When Henry VIII decided to abolish the Pope's authority in England and seize the assets of the church – hoping to solve both his financial and marital difficulties – public opinion was largely favourable and Henry was able to crush those who opposed him.

Wilton Abbey had again been in disarray for some time. In 1528 with scandal surrounding the election of a new abbess, Cardinal Wolsey sent Thomas Benet to Wilton to impose discipline, in particular the enclosure rules. But the nuns rebelled and gave Thomas Benet a hard time. Exasperated, he locked up the ringleaders and reported to the Cardinal that 'in no wise any of them by gentle means nor by rigorous – and I have put three of four of the captains of them in ward – will agree and consent to the same'.

In 1535 Thomas Leigh was sent to make another attempt at reform. He found the abbey in debt and with heavy charges including a scholarship for a student to each of the two universities, maintenance for thirteen 'Magdalens' and alms to the poor of the hospital of St Giles. Among many other less praiseworthy items of expenditure was an annual payment to the steward, the Earl of Shrewsbury, who at the time was nominally steward to 11 other monastic houses. Presumably in an attempt to mollify him – or under duress – in 1536 the abbess granted Thomas Leigh for one year the advowson of Stanton St Bernard. This gave him the right to nominate his own candidate to the comfortable job of prebendary, which came with a house in Wilton.

Closure could not be staved off and finally on 25th March 1539 the abbey surrendered to the king's commissioners. The abbess was granted a handsome pension of £100 a year together with a house and land in Fovant. There were pensions ranging from £7.6s.8d to £2 for the 31 nuns. The abbess had borrowed money to secure her election and after the closure the commissioners found that she had leased various abbey estates to her family and friends 'as was surmised'. She was however allowed to keep her settlement in Fovant.

7

The Earls of Pembroke

T HE ESTATES of the former Abbey of Wilton, including Stanton, were granted in 1544 to William Herbert, a skilled courtier who had been accumulating land and status even before he became the brother-in-law of King Henry VIII. William's wife Anne was the sister of Catherine Parr whom Henry had married the previous year. In 1551 William was created Earl of Pembroke by Edward VI. He had pulled down the 'ruinous' abbey at Wilton, replacing it with a fine new house where he entertained the young King Edward in 1552. William later managed to stay in favour with both the Catholic Queen Mary and the Protestant Queen Elizabeth I.

In 1563 the Earl commissioned a survey of his estates. In about 1904 this document, written in Latin on three rolls of vellum, was discovered in a wooden box in the gallery of the riding school at Wilton when workmen were 'clearing out a quantity of lumber, including old pieces of armour, mantel pieces, etc.'[75]

The Commissioners, Charles Vaughan and Robert Grove, had a lot of ground to cover, reporting on the Earl's estates in Devon, Somerset, Hampshire and Wiltshire. They visited Stanton on Tuesday 8th April 1567. They were not required to get their boots dirty surveying the land in the modern sense. Their work was done at a special meeting of the manor court, where they examined the records kept by the court and required tenants to present evidence of their holdings. Nineteen surnames are mentioned.[76] As always, the commissioners' primary interest was in the revenue the Pembroke estate could get from the land and there is therefore no information about the craftsmen and the farm workers who were not landholders.

Areas of land quoted are based on written information, sometimes many years old, but the field names are given.

The survey begins by listing the 5 areas of woodland: East Coppice, Mylway, Thornes, Esterbushe and Setton, totalling 84 acres. In the downland country, wood was a scarce but vital resource. Wood was the property of the lord of the manor and the copses were enclosed by hedges or fences. Pigs were often permitted to forage in the woods which also may have provided cover for game.

The freehold estate in Stanton, still held 'for a knight's fee', was divided at that time between William Unwin (sometimes spelt Unyon) and William Burdon. Between them they had grazing rights for 37 pigs, 42 cattle, 5 draught animals (either oxen or horses) and 300 sheep. They paid a total of 51s 6d to the lord of the manor (William Unwin paying 44s 6d and William Burdon 7s).

The former desmesne – the 'mansion' and 'farm of Stanton' – was held by Anthony Prater and his two brothers by indenture[77] for their lives, paying rent of £17 plus 30 fleeces. Their livestock included 22 oxen and they had grazing rights for 1000 sheep.

There were 16 copyhold[78] tenants, including Richard Hamlen at Stanton Mill whose rent was 43s10d. He had 6 draught animals, 15 cattle and grazing rights for 300 sheep on the hills and for 125 in the common fields.

The other tenants ranged from John Burdon whose rent was 36s 2d (and who had 6 draught animals, 14 cattle and grazing rights for 45 sheep on the hills and 125 in the common fields) down to Jana Dyer and her son Simon who had two animals and paid 4s for a cottage and 5 acres of land.

The rectory was leased for 21 years to Richard Hichcok, the Prebendary or Rector, and was valued at £20. He had grazing rights for 100 sheep and a horse, 10 cows and 10 pigs. He kept the only bull mentioned. The rector's holding included a 'well built house in Mynster Street with a garden and 1 rod of ground' in Wilton. This originated at the time when the Prebendary lived in Wilton to officiate at church services for the nuns of Wilton Abbey.

Stoniford Mill had not been included in the grant of the Stanton estate to William Herbert and at the time of

Detail of window at Mill Farm

the survey it was owned by the crown, having been granted to Queen Elizabeth before her accession. The tenants were the heirs of Sir Thomas Moyle.

The survey mentions 88 draught animals, 77 pigs and 228 other beasts, probably cattle. Altogether there were grazing rights for 1,650 sheep on the hills and on the lowland pasture. Animals were smaller at this time than their modern counterparts. Oxen were still used being for ploughing but on the lighter soils were gradually replaced with horses which were quicker and more manoeuvrable.

Daily life was characterised by constant movement of people and of animals within the village and on the surrounding land: people walking to and from their work, moving with their tools between their dispersed strips of land in the common fields, people doing their daily tasks in the gardens and orchards in the village, visiting the carpenter and the blacksmith, people carrying things, stopping to gossip, driving animals through the village, pedlars arriving with their wares on their backs or on pack-horses, people taking their produce to market, people walking to church on Sundays and on saints' days, visiting their friends, walking to the alehouse in the evenings. And every day, morning and evening, the sound of sheep bells as the flocks were moved between the hills and the fields.

A small community is seldom an idyllic place and life in Stanton was marred for 20 years or so by the activities of the quarrelsome Anthony Prater who, as holder of the former desmesne farm, was a powerful man in the village and came from a rich family with land in Somerset. He seems to have had a running feud with John Burden in particular but caused trouble generally. He appeared before the courts several times, clashed with the Earl of Pembroke's agents and was excommunicated by the church. At the Midsummer Sessions in 1586 he was bound over to keep the peace 'particularly towards John Burden' for the sum of £10 and summoned to appear at the next session. He died, still unreconciled to the church, in 1593 and was remembered as a 'troublesome man'. Numerous descendants of the Praters are now in the USA and Anthony would probably relish the fact that he features on at least two American family history websites.

In 1603 the vicar, William Cromwell, petitioned the 'Justices of the County of Wilts' for assistance for Alice Haynes, a widow whose property had been destroyed by fire:

> That whereas by misfortune of fyer suddainly ariseing in and upon the fouth day of November laste paste between tenne and eleven of the clock at nyghte the parsonage house at Stanton aforesaid wherein the said widdowe and her poore children did their dwell was burned and all her goodes and household stufe in the

same house to the value of twentie pounds was then and there by the same fyre quite wasted and consumed to the utter improvershinge and undoinge of the said poore widdowe and her six small children. . . May it therefore pleae yor worshippes to have compassion upon the poore distressed widdowe being nowe in a woful case and to allow some portion of that money wich is collected with the County Courts for such Charitable uses as in yor worshipful consideracons shall be (–) good towards the relief of the afflicted widdowe and her poore children . . . and for that it maye more playnlie unto yor worshipps that this is true the pties whose names are under written being inhabitants of the said pishe have putt their handes . . .[79]

The signatures were those of William Cromwell, Christopher Baylye, Palle Samson, William Godwyn and Richard Plooth. William Cromwell had been vicar of Stanton since 1569 and died in 1604.

In the Middle Ages the Church, and in particular the monastic houses, provided care for the sick and assistance for the poor. After the dissolution of the monasteries individual parishes were made responsible for the relief of the poor under the Poor Law Acts of 1563 and 1601. Two or more Overseers of the Poor were appointed in each parish to act with the Church Wardens and were empowered to raise taxes for the maintenance of paupers. The old or sick were given their 'parish relief' whilst other paupers and 'sturdy beggars' were expected to earn theirs by doing menial tasks, for which raw materials could be provided. Orphans or children whose parents could not support them were apprenticed. This system remained in force until the 19th century.

With the estates of Wilton Abbey, the Earls of Pembroke had acquired the right to nominate prebendaries who in turn nominated vicars to serve in their parishes. Henry Herbert, the second Earl, gave the prebend of Stanton to Robert Parker, a leading theologian and prominent puritan. Parker's strong views were unpalatable to King James I who offered a reward for his capture, whereupon Parker took refuge in Holland. Robert Parker's son Thomas, also a staunch puritan, is said to have been born in Stanton.[80] In 1633 Thomas emigrated to America, becoming one of the founders of the town of Newbury, Massachusetts. The Parker River is named after him.[81]

On the death of William Cromwell in 1604, Robert Parker's nominee Richard Stevens, a Presbyterian, succeeded him as vicar of Stanton. He set up the first recorded school in Stanton which was held in the chancel of the church. Richard's son Nathaniel was born in the village in 1606 and according to some manuscript notes found in the church safe in Stanton, used to tell the following story:

> A clergyman, coming into the secluded village church, advanced towards the chancel
> in order to bow at the altar. But Stanton St Bernard could not yet boast of an altar,
> for a Communion table, on a modest level with the rest of the flooring, occupied
> its place against the east wall, and upon this table a village lad was sitting, no better
> employed than 'kicking his heels'.
>
> Perceiving the figure approaching him, the boy slipped down and stood
> before the table. At length the priest made a low bow and the honest rustic thinking
> it was to himself that the homage was paid, bowed as low to him again; and the
> bows were repeated three times on each side, the boy being greatly surprised at
> such unwonted civility in a priest.
>
> 'In this case', Mr Stevens would say, 'the boy knew well enough who it was
> be bowed to, but whether it was so with the priest is questionable, for the object
> of a Christian's worship is no more to be discovered in the East than in the West –
> no more in the chancel than in the church – nor in the church more than in the
> dwelling house or green fields unless when his people are there worshipping him
> in spirit and in truth.'

With the vicar holding views like these, the lad probably thought of the chancel more as a schoolroom than a church.

Nathaniel was later vicar of Drayton in Leicestershire where he met George Fox, the founder of the Quaker movement, who initially influenced him greatly. However their views eventually diverged. Their relationship ended in a very public row when Fox entered the church where Nathaniel was preaching and tried to shout him down. Nathaniel called out that Fox was mad and the congregation turned on Fox and drove him out of the church.[82]

Richard Stevens was vicar of Stanton from 1604 to 1660, the turbulent period from the reign of James I through the Civil War and the Commonwealth to the return of King Charles II. He maintained his puritanical views and in 1646 wrote a petition for the suppression of ale houses as: 'tending to the great dishonour of God, the prophanation of the Sabbath, the breaches of many ordinances of Parliament, the maintenance of riots, poverty, idleness of living.'[83]

Village alehouses were often run by women who brewed the beer and sold it in their houses. At a time when living conditions at home were cramped and fuel and lighting expensive, the attractions of the alehouse are obvious but for centuries they were fiercely criticised and attacked by the clergy.

In 1631 the 4th Earl of Pembroke, who had succeeded his father the previous year, commissioned another survey which gives a brief description of the tenants' houses and farm buildings in addition to the usual details of their landholdings and grazing rights. The rent and the age of the tenant or tenants were carefully noted. People held their land for terms of two or three 'lives', the tenancy passing from father to son, or husband to widow, on payment of a 'fine' to the landowner together with a 'heriot', usually of 'the best beast'. With rents often relatively low, landowners made their money from the fines. Frustratingly, there is no accompanying map so it is not usually possible to identify exactly where the named tenants lived in the village.

In the 64 years which had elapsed between the surveys, the pattern of land tenure had remained constant: there were two large holdings, the freehold farm and the former desmesne farm, and the number of copyholders had increased from 16 to 18. The main change was the enclosure of some of the common meadows and pasture to the benefit of the largest landholders, giving them exclusive grazing rights there. This was the start of the process of enclosure which would in time make the smaller copyhold tenancies unviable.

The freeholder was John Boothe, gentleman, holding 11 yardlands[84] by a 'knight's fee' (an ancient form of tenure dependent on military service). He had 174 acres of arable in the common fields, over 45 acres of meadow and pasture plus grazing rights for 300 sheep on the downs. He had 'a dwelling house, 3 barns, 2 stables, a cow house and a dove house which, with the backsides, gardens and orchard and closes all lying about the house, contain in all 10 acres'.

By this time the Praters had left Stanton and the 'site, mansion place and farm of Stanton' was held by Joan Baskerville aged 44, the widow of Thomas Baskerville, esquire, who had been a Justice of the Peace. The fine payable by a new tenant was the enormous sum of £500 with a heriot of £3. 6s. 8d. The rent was still £17, plus 30 fleeces and 3 quarters of wheat to be delivered to Ramsbury at Christmas. The land was valued at £220 and was 'reputed 20 yardlands'. The house was 'of 6 ground rooms lofted over' and there was an old brew house of 3 ground rooms, 2 barns consisting of 10 bays and 2 porches, 2 stables, an ox house, a cart house, a backside, garden and orchard (in all covering 7 acres).

The holdings of the 18 copyhold tenants were more modest, between 1 and 3 yardlands each. Most had houses with three or four 'ground rooms, lofted over', with gardens, orchards, barns and other farm buildings. The only person with less than 1 yardland was Edward Hibberd, aged 65 and his daughters Ann (24) and Christian (22) who paid 4s for a house with 3 ground rooms, 2 of them lofted over, a small barn, and a garden and orchard of ¼ acre in all. They had 4½ acres of arable land, just over 1 acre of pasture and grazing rights for 2 sheep in the common fields and wastes.

The second largest copyhold tenancy was that of Geffrey Burdon, as he signed himself in his will. An individual's name could appear in many different forms due to the erratic spelling of the time. He was a descendant of Robert Burdon who held the freehold farm in the 13th century. Geffrey, carrying his copy of the entry in the court roll of 1629 which gave him title to his land, would certainly have been present on 19th May 1631 at the meeting in Stanton of the Court of Survey. Geffrey and his fellow tenants were well used to attending the regular meeting of the 'courts baron' where the agricultural routine of the village was discussed and agreed. But this meeting, presided over by the Earl's commissioners, Robert Drewe and William Kent, was more formal and more daunting.

By the time of the survey, Geffrey was 52 years old and had a holding of 3 yardlands (about 60 acres) with his brother William (48) and William's son Andrew (20). It was the land held by John Burdon at the time of the 1567 survey. The annual rent was 36s 2¾d, with a fine of £80 following a death and a heriot of the two best beasts and a small money payment. The holding was valued at £40. Geffrey had 50 acres of arable land in strips dispersed around the common fields: 22¼ acres in the North Field 'above the town' and 27¾ acres in South Field 'below the town. Each year one of these fields would lie fallow so he would have roughly half his arable land under cultivation at any time.

He was allowed to graze 14 or 15 cattle (in alternate years) and 6 horses in the common fields when they lay fallow. The horses could also be tethered to feed in the designated 'baiting places'. To provide additional fodder, Geffrey had three fenced areas of meadow land (totalling about 6 acres) in East Meads, West Meads and Horseballs located in the wetter area south of the village, and could cut hay from part of the Lammas meadow 'according to the order of the fields'. He had a 'fodderhouse' and a close of pasture in Moores, also in the south of the parish. He had grazing rights for 45 sheep on the downs and for 126 in the common fields and wastes. His sheep would join the village flocks under the care of the shepherds employed by the parish.

The Wiltshire Quarter Sessions set out maximum rates for wages in the county in 1655. This was an attempt to stabilise the situation after the Civil War, but it gives some indication of the wages Geffrey would have been paying. The inference is that these rates were being widely exceeded at the time. The maximum annual wage for a 'common servant of husbandry' was £3, and for women servants it was £1 10s 0d. Day labourers employed on mowing grass or reaping wheat and rye got a maximum of 8d per day with food and drink or 16d without, whilst haymakers rated 6d or 10d. Hedgers, ditchers and threshers got no more than 3d per day in winter and 4d in summer with food and drink, or 7d and 8d without.

If Geffrey had animals to sell, they could be driven the short distance to Tan Hill Fair held every summer. A visit to the Fair, with its market stalls and the bustle of people coming from far afield would be one of the highlights of the year for Geffrey and his relatives as well as for their servants. At other times of the year, buying and selling could be done at the market in Devizes.

With the help of the 1784 map of the parish it is possible to see where Geffrey lived. The survey states that he had a 'dwelling house of 4 ground rooms, 3 lofted over', 2 barns (one of 4 bays, the other of 3 and a porch) and a backside, a garden and an orchard 'augmented with a close called Thornes'. On the map *Thorns Close* is behind the present-day Corner Cottage, and is bounded by Coate Road (known as *Thorns Lane* in the 18th century) and by the lane now leading to the Old Rectory. Geffrey had two closes of pasture near his house: *Dog Lands* (the field to the north of *Laburnum Cottage* and *Reads Close*), and *Broad Close* across the road from his house (adjacent to *Church Walk*). *Broad Close* was also called *Rob Close* in the survey and Geffrey had a cottage known as *Rob Croft*. Pigs, bees, geese and pigeons could have been reared, and there could have been apple and cherry trees in the orchard[85] .

Farmhouses from this period survive in the village today (for example *Sarsens* and *Laburnum Cottage*), but Geffrey's house has disappeared. During the late 16th and early 17th centuries the climate became colder and houses were built with greater comfort in mind. The major innovation was the chimney which replaced the open fire in the middle of the room. Cruck construction was largely abandoned, giving enough height to 'loft over' the ground floor rooms, creating usable rooms on the first floor. The inventory taken on 17th January 1659[86] after Geffrey's death lists his furniture and the contents of his house.

The wearing apparel	£6 0 0d
The bed and bedstead in the parlour	£4 0 0
The bed, board and chairs in the parlour	£0 5 0
The chest, table, board and bedstead in the chamber above the parlour, and bedding	£2 0 0
The bedding and trunk in the chamber above the hall	£2 10 0

The cheese	£0 12 0
The bed and bedstead in the chamber above the kitchen	£1 0 0
The brass and pewter	£4 0 0
The wooden vessels in the kitchen	£1 0 0
The bacon	£4 0 0
The barrels and safe	£1 2 0
The jack and spits	£0 8 0
The table, board, chairs, cupboard, forms and stool in hall	£1 0 0
The andirons, dog and fender	£0 5 0
The bullock	£0 15 0
The sheep	£10 0 0
The hay	£4 0 0
The corn in the barn	£12 10 0
The corn upon the ground	£10 10 0
The wood	£6 10 0
The fann (for winnowing) and quern (for grinding corn)	£0 10 0
The press (probably for cheese making)	£1 8 0
The garner (small barn for storing corn) and wooden boards	£1 17 0
Item his money	£80 0 0
Item his books	£20 0 0
	£216 10 0d

The ground floor rooms were the hall, used for eating and entertaining, the parlour which was being used as sleeping quarters, and the kitchen. Geffrey's house had a fourth ground floor room, probably next to the kitchen and which could have contained a bread oven or was possibly used for cheese-making or storage. Cheeses and sometimes also the valuable stock of bacon, were often kept in one of the upstairs rooms. The jack and spits for roasting meat would be used in the kitchen and the 'andirons, dog and fender' were the fire irons in the hall fireplace. Beds were four-posters with curtains to keep out the draught, often with a truckle bed stowed underneath which was pulled out for use by children or servants. Feather beds were a luxury which had recently made their appearance. Geffrey was 82 when he died and there is no record of him having been married or having children. The number of beds listed indicates that Geffrey's relatives were living in the house with him at the end of his life.

This was the typical house of a prosperous yeoman farmer, comfortably furnished. The unusual feature is the large quantity of books. Geffrey was a close

Examples of furniture and household items of the period of Geffrey Burdon's inventory

friend of the vicar, Richard Stevens, and was clearly a studious man, interested in religious matters. The £80 in cash in the house is exactly the sum needed to pay the fine for the change of tenancy and indicates some foresight on Geffrey's part.

Geffrey's inventory was taken by his nephew, John Smith, and by his fellow copyholders Christopher Platt, Samuel Hamlon and Richard Lavington who was probably acting in his capacity as tithingman (constable).

In his will dated 23rd April 1659 Geffrey makes the following bequests:

Item I give unto my nephew Andrew Burdon his son John my book called Sir
Edward Cooke's Commentary on Littleton and my gold ring.

Item I forgive my niece Susan Ansell forty shillings that she borrowed of me.

Item I forgive the Executors of Richard Farmer that they owe me.

Item I give unto John Smith the son of Daniel Smith five pounds, and to Elizabeth
Smith his sister ten pounds and a feather bed.

Item I give unto Daniel Smith the son of Daniel Smith eight pounds and to his
brothers Timothy and Isaac forty shillings apiece.

Item I give unto the poor of our parish ten shillings to be disposed by my Overseer.

The rest of my goods I give unto my niece Elizabeth Smith and to Gefferey Smith
her son whom I make executors of this my last will and testament, entreating
my true friend Mr Richard Stevens our vicar to be the Overseer of this my
last will and testament. . .

The Will is witnessed by Christopher Platt, Samuel Hamlon and Richard Stevens.

Geffrey left ten shillings to pay for his burial within the church. His tombstone can still be seen in the floor under the window in the south wall opposite the double doors, partially hidden by a cupboard. Two Latin phrases testify to his piety and learning but victim to the last of lax spelling, he is commemorated as 'Jefferie Burtdon'.

8

Civil War and Two Legacies

G EFFREY BURDON and his neighbours lived through the Civil War. What their opinions were and which side they supported is not known but the presence of a puritan vicar must have coloured their outlook. At the start of the war in 1642 the supporters of Parliament took control in the greater part of Wiltshire and garrisoned the towns, including Devizes, Marlborough and Salisbury.

The 5th Earl of Pembroke took the parliamentary side. He was Parliament's Lord Lieutenant of Wiltshire for a short period and was responsible in 1642 for completing the organisation of the county militia. He was a member of various delegations sent to negotiate with Charles I. Perhaps as a result of this frustrating experience he gained a reputation for swearing and was lampooned in a satirical pamphlet in which the word 'D . . ned' appeared very frequently. Wilton House was occupied and damaged by the royalists but the Earl got little gratitude from his own side. He was one of seven lords accused in Parliament of high treason, apparently because he did not go off to fight. He protested that he was old and had been active taking 'propositions' to the King. He died in 1649, the year of the King's execution.

With the King's headquarters in Oxford and with military action taking place throughout the west country, Wiltshire suffered the effects of the armies of both sides frequently passing through, as well as from the actual fighting. In November 1642, Marlborough fell to the royalists, who set fire to part of the town and sacked houses and shops. The royalists occupied Devizes after the withdrawal of the parliamentary garrison in February 1643 and began to gain the upper hand.

The King's Cornish army under General Hopton took refuge in Devizes on 9th July after their defeat by General Waller's force at Lansdown. Waller pursued them and laid siege to the town, occupying Roundway Hill. The royalists, intent on relieving the town, were assembling a cavalry force under Henry Wilmot in Marlborough and sending supplies and reinforcements from Oxford. Waller's scouts warned him of this and on 10th July he sent out a detachment which captured 200 men and an ammunition train of 'four waynes of powder and one of bullet and match' at Alton. Waller's batteries at Coatfields outside Devizes 'poured great and small shot into the town' for the next two days.

Henry Wilmot's force from Marlborough approached Devizes early on 13th July. They fired two cannon shots when they reached Bishops Cannings Down, a pre-arranged signal to the royalists besieged in Devizes that relief was at hand and they should break out of the town. However, Hopton thought this was a ruse of Waller's and did not respond. Waller's army formed up on Roundway Down. His cavalry faced a ferocious onslaught from the royalist cavalry which sent them fleeing to destruction down the steep slope of Roundway Hill. Hopton's troops finally came out from Devizes and Waller's infantry was overwhelmed.

The disastrous defeat at Roundway Down was a low point in the fortunes of Parliament, causing its leaders to reappraise the organisation and training of its troops. The result was the creation of Cromwell's New Model Army which brought victory to the Parliamentary side. Devizes remained in royalist hands until it was recaptured by Cromwell in September 1645.

For Stanton people, the war had come uncomfortably close, particularly the skirmish at Alton. From the beginning of the war, both sides were recruiting men into their armies and as the war dragged on their methods became more brutal. Both sides quickly became very short of money and set up County Committees in the areas under their control to organise the collection of taxes. The disruption of trade by the war added to people's financial difficulties. The garrison commanders were also exacting money and supplies of food, fodder and services from the surrounding countryside. Armies passing through billeted their men in the villages and country houses and made similar demands, sometimes carrying off horses and the stocks of food from the barns. There are no records to show whether troops were billeted in Stanton before the battle of Roundway but the parish registers of Alton Barnes contain these entries:

. . . to be paid by virtue of warrant and command from my Lord Marquis of
Hartford for bread and hay for his army at the Devizes, July 11th 1643 – 8s.

paid for shoeing of horses of Lord Wilmott and his troops July 13th 1643, who
lay in both Altons then – 10s. (This was the day of the battle of Roundway)

When the forces of King Charles came this way to fight . . . the suff imposed on
Alton Barnes (for his soldiers) July 15th 1643 totalled £8.9s.0d.

Taxation was levied on the basis of the Hundreds and it is certain that Stanton
would have paid its share. Tithingmen were responsible for collecting and paying
taxes locally. Warrants sent to them could be threatening in tone 'weekly payment
hereafter without further warrant hereof, you are not to fayle at your peril'. The
money was to be paid 'at the Crowne at the Devizes'. After the war, taxes were
levied to pay for the damage. In 1650, as tithingman, Richard Lavington of Stanton
made the payment, probably for both parishes, and in the following year he was
collector for a fund 'for reparation of the bridge at Sarum'.[87]

With its strongly nonconformist vicar, Richard Stevens, Stanton probably
experienced little change during the Commonwealth era. Richard Stevens died in
1660, the year of the Restoration of Charles II. Charles II banned the printing of
nonconformist books and pamphlets and in some places nonconformist vicars
were removed from their livings, but on the whole he fostered a more tolerant
atmosphere. Thomas Crapon who became vicar in 1665 had been ejected from his
living in Fifield Bavant in 1662 and so presumably continued the low church
tradition in Stanton which was in tune with the general feeling in the area.

A sad incident is recorded by Warden Woodward of New College, Oxford,
on one of his visits to Alton Barnes. Mr Budd, the vicar of Alton Barnes, was
following the official church policy of the time towards suicides.

April 1665: Henry Apes, a youth under 20 years old, servant unto William Stone
of Alton Barnes in the county of Wilts did then in the barn of the said William
Stone hang himself, sometime in the morning. His goods in all came to 30s., but
of which, when they had paid the coroner, brought him a shroud, and prepared
for his burial, there remained five shillings and a little bible. The bible his friends
desired, the 5s remaining were paid unto the College at the audit 1666. The evidence
of the young man's hanging himself may been seen in the coroners office at the
Devizes. He was buried between the two parishes of Staunton and Alton Barnes,
with two stakes thrust through him. Mr Budd would not suffer him to be buried
in the churchyard nor is he entered into the book of burials.

Warden Woodward regularly visited Alton and the other estates in Wiltshire owned by New College between 1659 and 1675. He kept a close eye on the use of timber and carefully monitored requests from tenants for timber for repairs and for new farm buildings, checking that they had used the wood for the purpose intended and not sold it. After the Restoration he was asked for a tree to make a maypole and admits being beguiled by the village girls into granting one.

At the end of the 17th century there was increasing poverty in the countryside. The 1697 Act of Settlement decreed that paupers could only claim relief in the parish in which they had been born or were officially deemed to have 'settled'. This gave Overseers licence to send paupers back to villages which in some cases they had left many years ago. The new Game Laws prohibiting the taking of any kind of game prevented the poor from supplementing their meagre food supply in the traditional way.

However there were fortunes to be made elsewhere. In 1660 Thomas Fowle had finished his apprenticeship and set up his own business as a master goldsmith in Fleet Street in London. In the year of the Restoration life held exciting new possibilities for young people. Thomas had been born in Stanton in 1637, one of the five sons of Edward Fowle, yeoman. Edward knew that his farm could not support all his sons, so he arranged for the three youngest, Daniel, Robert and Thomas, to be apprenticed to London goldsmiths.

Thomas thrived in the bustling London of Charles II, Christopher Wren and Samuel Pepys. He sold jewellery and plate to the gentry, to the lawyers who worked in the City and to members of the Court at Westminster. He also developed a lucrative banking business. After a slight check in 1665 when he had to shut down his business for 5 months during the Great Plague, in June 1666 he married Jane Norton, daughter of a prosperous stationer who brought him a wedding portion of £900. When the Fire of London broke out in September of that year, Thomas's luck held: the direction of the wind changed just before the fire reached his premises. Other goldsmiths were not so fortunate and many lost their buildings and stock. In 1667 Thomas and his brother Robert became liverymen of the Goldsmiths' Company.

In 1674 Thomas arranged an apprenticeship for his nephew William, born in Stanton and son of his elder brother Edward who had stayed on the family farm. William proved to be an exceptionally talented silversmith with a gift for design. As soon as William completed his apprenticeship in 1681, Thomas set him up in his own business and commissioned work from him. Among the objects William produced were magnificent silver-gilt toilet sets. They consist of a number of boxes

Pincushion from the Calverley Toilet set

and brushes with a tray and a framed mirror, all elaborately chased and embossed. His 'Calverley' toilet set is now in the Victoria and Albert Museum and another was sold by Christies in 2003 to an American museum, at an estimated price of US$500,000. William died tragically young after a short illness in 1684. He has been described as 'a remarkable young silversmith who may now be seen to have produced some of the finest pieces of English silver that survive from the late Stuart period'.

Thomas continued to prosper, particularly in his banking business. He was knighted in 1686, was made an Alderman of the City of London and served as Sheriff. However, he was turning his thoughts to his native Wiltshire and was buying property there. In 1690 Thomas decided to stand for Parliament in the Devizes constituency. Towns at that time returned two members and on this occasion there were three candidates: Thomas, John Methuen and Walter Grubbe. Only burgesses living in the town were eligible to vote. Fifty-nine of them appeared at the poll and elected Walter Grubbe and John Methuen. However the mayor, Richard Hiller, had other ideas and 'took upon himself privately' to persuade eight burgesses, not resident in Devizes and having no right to vote, to be polled for Thomas. Using his own seal, not the official seal of the Corporation, the mayor returned Walter Grubbe and Sir Thomas Fowle as MPs for Devizes.

John Methuen objected to this outcome and petitioned the House of Commons. At the first session of the House the matter was referred to the Committee of Privileges, along with over 30 other similar complaints about election irregularities. Surprisingly, the Committee upheld the election of Thomas and Walter Grubbe.

Thomas had bought a manor in Pewsey, property in Fyfield and Lockeridge and in 1691 the freehold farm in Stanton. He did not have long to enjoy his land and his parliamentary career. He died on 11th November 1692 aged 55 in London and

Detail of door at Manor Farm House

was buried in St Dunstans-in-the-West in the City of London, having stipulated in his will[88] that if he died in Wiltshire, he was to be buried in the church of 'Stanton Barnard'. His daughter Susan and her husband Jonathon Cope inherited the farm in Stanton.

Thomas had not forgotten his origins and the opportunity that his apprenticeship had given him to make his fortune as a craftsman. Wanting to give others the same chance in life, in his Will he gave 'to the poore of the parish of Stanton Barnard in Wiltshire where I was borne fifty pounds to bee a Stock to put out poore Children to Trade or Calling'.

About thirty years later a similar bequest was made by another Stanton man, Isaac Smith, a tailor in the City of London. Little is known about Isaac who, like Thomas Fowle, was one of several sons of a Stanton yeoman farmer and was sent to London to serve his apprenticeship. Isaac died in May 1720, evidently a successful man but not as wealthy as Thomas Fowle. In his Will[89] he names his four brothers and a long list of relatives, most of whom each receive one shilling; a few get twenty shillings

Detail of chimney from Manor Farm House

and the lucky minority £10. He makes several bequests for the poor – mostly of 40 shillings – but by far the most generous is one to Stanton, the second largest in the Will: 'I give to the parish of Stanton Barnard twenty pounds for the use towards the putting poor Boys prentice'.

These two bequests together form the Fowle and Smith Charity, which is still in existence. In 1779 the trustees invested the money in just over 3 acres[90] of land, which the charity still owns, in All Cannings parish to the west of the road leading out of the village from the church. In 1829 the land was divided up into allotments and let to Stanton people, providing the charity with income from the rents. Very soon there was a waiting list for the allotments, which were chiefly used to grow potatoes. When the ground became 'potato sick' the allotments were moved to land in the centre of the village, and the charity received the rent from them. Now the charity's income comes from the rent paid for the use of its land in All Cannings for agriculture.

Today the Fowle and Smith Charity offers grants to Stanton children leaving school for textbooks for further education or for the tools and clothing needed when they start work.

9

Mrs Wyndham and Mrs Church

A N ENERGETIC new Vicar arrived in Stanton in 1728, Rev. Thomas Smith. On 5th May 1729 he notes in the Parish Register that he 'began taking down the Vicaridge House' which was then near the church, on the site of the present village hall. Construction of the new vicarage on the same site began on 27th June 1729. Rev. Smith was Vicar of Stanton until 1760 and during his time it seems that the church became less austere. The gifts, from 'a person unknown', of a scarlet pulpit cloth and a cushion in 1746 and of a 'bason for the font' in 1748 are recorded in the Parish Register.

On 25th March 1744 (which under the pre-1752 calendar was New Year's day) the Vicar drew up 'An Account of the Souls within this Parish'. The document is torn at the bottom and the entry for one household is incomplete. He lists 58 households, containing at least 143 adults and 104 children under 16.

The Vicar was not entirely a man of peace, as appears from the 'Justicing Notebook' kept by William Hunt, Justice

Detail from Andrews and Dury's 1773 map

of the Peace, who heard cases from the Swanborough Hundred at *The Horse and Jockey* in West Lavington, usually sitting with another JP. The Justices seem to have done their best to reconcile the parties but if necessary, cases were referred to the Quarter Sessions. On 29th August 1746 a warrant was granted: ' at the complaint of Rev. Mr Thomas Smith of Staunton Bernard against John Hobbs of the same parish, butcher, for his stamping upon the feet of the said Mr Smith.' John Hobbs was bound to appear at the Quarter Sessions at Marlborough in October 1746 where the case was dismissed. The following year, on 22nd July, the Vicar made a complaint against Henry Mede and John Tucker:

> touching in particular the said John Tucker's illegally entertaining the aforesaid Henry Mede and suffering him to sit tippling in his house, and the said Henry Mede for so tippling in the same house, and for other abuses to the said Mr Smith against the peace. Dismissed upon hearing for want of evidence. Henry Mede of Staunton Bernard convicted on oath for swearing in the hearing of two justices of the peace 17 Sept 1747.

The Justices sometimes charged a man with swearing when they had insufficient evidence to convict him of another offence of which he was strongly suspected. The Vicar was not the only litigant. In the same month Nathaniel Ricks, the miller, accused two women labourers, Bridget Higgens and Mary Taylor, of stealing household goods from his house but the case was dismissed 'for want of proof, the charge being false against the parties'. William Hunt's notebook contains many accusations of theft and those of food and of wood in the winter in particular reveal the depth of poverty in which many people were living.

As they had since the Middle Ages, the Manor Courts continued to meet in Stanton, possibly in a building near the present Church Farm. The 1784 map shows a 'Court Gate' and path leading to that site. By the 18th century the meetings were held annually, attended generally by 6 to 8 men, and the records are mostly repetitions of 'customs of the manor' which presumably reflect infringements reported.[91] Two Tellers of Sheep were appointed each year, together with a Hayward who supervised the use of the common land. Many entries deal with grazing and folding rights:

> After every person that have sheep in the tenantry flock at Down have had their due proportion of nightsfold in the Common Fields of this Manor (that is to say seven nights to 30 sheep) the same Down sheep ought to be folded on the Down until they go to fodder.

No one ought to turn their pigs out into the Common fields unless they are first ringed and do order the Hayward to impound all such pigs as he shall find there not being ringed and to be paid 6d apiece for the same.

The Lammas ground and stubble fields ought to be fed with the horses 9 days before the sheep and no longer according to the custom of the Manor.

There were complaints about individuals: Mary Cromwell and Catherine Perry, widows, for enclosing part of the common; Simon Pile for driving and folding his sheep in the Summer Field before May Day, 'he having no right thereto'; William Lydall for planting trees against the boundaries of John Fowle. The Vicar was reminded that according to custom he 'ought to keep a bull for the use of the tenants' cows of this Manor'.

Changes of tenancy were recorded and tenants' rights and obligations were reiterated, including the custom that if both husband and wife were admitted as tenants, on the death of one, the survivor had the right to take over the tenancy.

All tenants were expected to meet once a year to walk the bounds of the Manor and the bounds of the Common Fields, and were fined 1s if they did not attend. Rights of way were also a constant concern:

Church Path is no road for carts, wagons or horses and that everyone trespassing in going that way as aforesaid shall forfeit and pay 1s.

The Long Rudgeway is no Horse Road and that every person who shall offend in going that way with Horses shall forfeit and pay 5s.

No right of footway over the Tenantry field from Rings Gate to the grounds of Little Mead – fine 1s for trespass.

The right of the Drove belonging to the Down sheep is in or through the Barley Field until Old May Day yearly and there is no right of drove in the Summer field until that time.

These entries give a flavour of the many rules designed to ensure the smooth running of the communal farming routine. Although they were recorded in the court book, the 'customs of the manor' and the location and ownership of the different fields and strips formed a vast body of knowledge which people needed to carry in their heads in order to perform their daily tasks.

It was now time for changes to be made. The population was growing steadily, food was scarce and it became necessary to start importing grain during the second half of the 18th century. The old ridge and furrow system was now seen as an obstacle to implementing more efficient agricultural practices. Crop rotation was found to be more productive than allowing land to lie fallow. The system of folding animals in the common fields at specified times limited the variety of crops which could be grown. There was an interest in selective breeding to improve livestock and this could not be done when the village animals all grazed together on the common pasture.

Enclosure was thought to be the answer: allocating to each tenant fields equivalent in area to the strips he had held in the common fields and ending the system of communal grazing. This process had been happening on a smaller scale since the early 17th century, but from the middle of the 18th century it became widespread. In parishes where there were a number of landowners an Act of Parliament was often necessary but in Stanton enclosure was carried out by agreement in 1792. By then the Earl of Pembroke owned the whole of the Stanton estate. In 1724 Francis Hawes, a Director of the South Sea Company, was negotiating the purchase of the freehold farm just at the time when the 'South Sea Bubble' collapsed. The farm, known as 'Little Farm', was sold at an auction of the Directors' assets held at South Sea House in 1726 and was bought by the Pembroke Estate.

In preparation for enclosure, a survey was made in 1784/5[92] with a map showing the ridge and furrow system, each strip marked with a code indicating the holder. This time the surveyors actually measured the land, including the areas of the roads, and expressed the result in acres, rods and perches, not in vague and archaic terms such as 'yardlands'. The survey shows that the pattern of landholding was changing from the two large farms and the 16 or 18 yeomen's holdings which had remained fairly constant from the time of Domesday to the 17th century. Now the yeomen's holdings were gradually decreasing in size and being absorbed into the larger farms.

For the first time the survey shows the 'cottages on the waste' which poorer people erected on spare pieces of land, often beside roads. There were 14 of these cottages, six of them on the triangle of land now occupied by *Lydnarda* and *New Woodlands Cottage*, at the junction of the north-south road through the village and the drove road from the hills. The Overseers of the Poor had one of the cottages on this site and another further up the drove road to use for homeless people, or to rent out to provide income for poor relief.

Roads were rather different in the 18th century: a note to the survey states that horses are allowed to graze on 'part of the Devizes Road from the Sand Pits westward to the outside of the Manor . . . from Old May Day to Lammas Day when the west field above the Town is sown with wheat'.

It is possible to see where some of the craftsmen lived. In the centre of the village where *Winford* now stands, Stephen Tasker had a blacksmith's shop and a house. The carpenters were John Hamlen on the site of *1 and 2 Hillview* and Thomas Springbatt at *Fowlers Lane Cottage*. Sadly in 1793 'Thomas Springbott moving and lifting ash timber with a lever was killed by a violent blow from the lever on his forehead'.[93] Samuel Hamlen also had a carpenter's shop at *2 Calf Lane* and was farming 30 acres of land. There was a shoemaker's shop and house on the site of *1 Reads Close*.

In addition to all their other work, the blacksmiths and the carpenters repaired and maintained the machinery in the two watermills in the south of the village. The grindstones were likely to have been made from Derby Peak millstone grit, or Buhrstone from France. To maintain the quality of the flour, the stones had to be dressed regularly. Specialist stone dressers travelled from mill to mill to do the job, which was arduous due to the hardness of the millstones.[94]

Daniel Hamlen held the 'Lower Mill' (Stanton Mill), described as an overshot grist mill,[95] which had been in his family since before 1563. He also held 19 acres of land. The records of the Manor state that it is the custom 'for all the Lord's tenants to grind their grist at the Lord's customary mill in Staunton belonging to Daniel Hamlon and he to fetch and carry back the same'. His house had three bedrooms and there was a barn, a carthouse and stable for 3 horses. Stoniford Mill was by now held by Simon Pile.

The survey indicates that there were watermeadows close to both mills. This was a system of irrigation designed to increase the supply of fresh grass in the early spring to feed sheep and lambs during the 'hungry gap' when stocks of hay

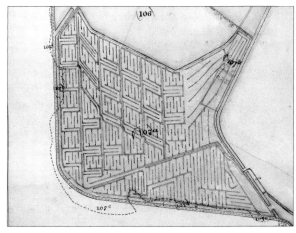

Watermeadows from the Pembroke Estate map of 1853

were exhausted. The meadows had to be levelled and a system of channels and sluices constructed to allow water from a nearby stream to cover the grass to a depth of a couple of inches. This kept the earth warm and promoted the early growth of the grass. The construction and management of watermeadows required special skills. The system had been developed in the 17th century and widely applied in the

18th, particularly on the Pembroke Estates.

Of the large landholders, Isaac Simpkins was now the tenant of Little Farm (about 197 acres) and was living in a house on the site of the *Old Rectory*. Thomas Dykes lived across the road from *Manor Farm House*: he had a substantial holding of 106 acres and a four-bedroomed house with two barns, outbuildings and stabling for 10 horses. Three people had holdings of about 60 acres: Thomas Walter at *Prices Cottage*, John Godwin living where *The Row* is now and Elizabeth Church on the site of *Greywethers*.

By far the wealthiest person in Stanton was Barbara Wyndham. Born Barbara Smith, she had inherited the tenancy of 'Great Farm' (as the old

Price's Cottage with nesting holes for doves

desmesne farm was now called) and had married William Wyndham whose rich and influential family played a prominent role in Wiltshire affairs. Barbara held over 785 acres, both *Manor Farm House* and the newly built *Church Farm House*, as well as a number of smaller houses.

The names of Mrs Wyndham and Mrs Church dominating Stanton on the 1773 map of the County of Wiltshire raise intriguing questions about their relationship: was it friendship or rivalry? Both were widows and although Elizabeth Church probably could not match Barbara Wyndham in terms of wealth, she was very well off, having land in Wootton Rivers as well as in Stanton. The publishers of the map, John Andrews and Andrew Dury, raised the money to print it by subscription. For 2½ guineas (£2 12s 6d), a subscriber received a copy of the map which, at a scale of 2' to 1 mile is very large, and had his name printed alongside a sketch representing his house. The roads marked on the map include those across the hills and in particular, the network converging on St Anne's Hill where Tan Hill Fair was held every year. It also reflects the growing interest in 'antiquities'. Standing stones and barrows are depicted, as well as the 'Old Monastery' of Avebury 'supposed by Antiquarians to be a Druid's Temple'. The map was designed to testify to the owner's culture and social standing.

During the 18th century, the gap between the poor and the better off had been widening. The enclosures accelerated this process. Enclosures were advantageous for the large landholders who were able to put into practice the new methods of agriculture. Initially some small farmers struggled to afford the new fences or hedges they were required to put up round the fields allocated to them.

In the long term most were unable to compete and their holdings were taken over by the larger farms. For smallholders who had been able to make a modest living on 4 or 5 acres with a few animals feeding on the common land, the loss of their grazing rights was a disaster.

In 1776 the Earl of Pembroke had appointed his former teacher at Harrow School, Rev. Thomas Bromley, to the living at Stanton. Bromley pocketed the Stanton tithes but continued his teaching career at Harrow, appointing Rev. Francis Rogers as curate of Stanton at a salary of £20 per year. Rogers was also deacon in Heddington. He lived in Stanton because the vicarage in Heddington was 'ruinous' and Stanton air was better for his wife's health. In the questionnaire he completed for the Bishop's 'visitation' in 1783, Rev. Rogers stated that he held Sunday services alternately in Stanton and Heddington due to his low pay and the bad roads. However he reported that there were very few people who did not go to church, no 'papists' in Stanton and only 'two or three deluded people called Methodists'. There was no church school in the village and little response when he tried to teach the catechism.[96]

The Methodists in the area had been growing in numbers ever since John Wesley's first tumultuous visit to Devizes in 1747. Later he again visited Devizes, Marlborough and the surrounding villages, drawing large and attentive audiences. There were other preachers, notably the Rev. Sloper, an 'Independent', in Devizes who inspired William Barrett to 'take the Gospel to the villages' which he did with great fervour. 'In the midst of winter' he was 'frequently obliged to preach out of doors on account of the number of hearers'. This did not go down well with the Bishop of Salisbury who put pen to paper. A 'war of pamphlets' ensued in 1798/9 known as the 'Salisbury village preaching controversy'.[97]

On 20th January 1798 a private house in Stanton was registered as an Independent meeting house and certified by William Barrett. Others named were William Williams, William Rabbetts, John Pope, Thomas Mills and A Jackson. The identity of the early nonconformist groups is not always clear: the Independents were also sometimes known as Congregationalists. In 1805 the

Thatched wall and gazebo at Manor Farm House

house occupied by William Ettwell, labourer, was registered for occasional use as a Methodist meeting house. Houses in All Cannings, Alton, Woodborough, Horton and Allington were also registered during this period.[98]

In 1806 the young Robert Tasker set out from his father's forge in Stanton and went to Abbotts Ann, near Andover, to work as assistant to another blacksmith, Thomas Maslen. In 1809 Robert took over Thomas Maslen's forge. With his brother William, Robert took advantage of the new technology pioneered in Ironbridge to develop an iron founding business which in time grew into Tasker & Sons Limited. Robert Tasker was a devout member of the Congregational Church and he and his successors looked after the welfare of their employees, providing houses, a school and a library. Specialising in agricultural implements, in the 1850s Taskers saw the possibilities of steam power and the company became famous for its traction engines and road rollers.

10

The Canal and Riots

ROUND THE TURN of the century there was a great deal of talk and speculation in the Vale of Pewsey about the canal. Work began on the Kennet and Avon Canal at Bradford in 1794. By 1799 the canal had reached the western side of Devizes and one of the sights of the town was the massive construction project of the 29 locks climbing Caen Hill, which took 10 years to complete. In 1803 work started on the Devizes to Pewsey section.

Stanton people watched with interest and some apprehension as the excavations slowly advanced along the Vale through All Cannings, crossed Stanton and then went on to Honey Street. There would have been rumours about the exploits of the gangs of navvies and perhaps some incidents in the village. Large numbers of men were needed and there were opportunities for employment for local men. The canal was dug using picks, shovels and wheelbarrows and was then lined with clay to make it watertight. While the construction work was going on life in the village would have been disrupted. Access to the mills and the south of the parish was difficult until the bricklayers and builders had completed the two bridges. This stretch of the canal was filled with water in the summer of 1806 and by the end of 1810 the Kennet and Avon Canal was complete and fully navigable, linking the Severn near Bristol to the Thames at Reading.[99] The boats pulled by plodding horses moving through the countryside were a novel sight.

In 1810 the Barge Inn was built on the parish border between Stanton and Honey Street to cater for the boatmen. It had a brew house, hop store, bake house, slaughterhouse, smoke house and cart shed. There was stabling for four horses.

The drove road from Stanton to Woodborough passed next to the Barge Inn and was now interrupted by the canal. The Canal Company, recognising its obligations, provided a boat. In the 1950s there was a floating bridge in the form of a pontoon, about 3 feet wide with a handrail on each side, moored at each end to an iron stake to enable it to be swung out of the way of passing boats, but by this time the canal had been closed to traffic. When the pontoon became unsafe, it was not replaced.

The Alton Barnes white horse, another familiar landmark, made its appearance in about 1812. Its originator was Robert Pile of Manor Farm, Alton Barnes, who paid £20 in advance to a journeyman painter called Jack Thorne to cut out the horse. Thorne is said to have prepared a drawing for the horse, sub-contracted the hard work to John Harvey of Stanton and disappeared with the money before the job was finished. The horse was completed in the end, and it is to be hoped that John Harvey got paid. Jack Thorne was later hanged for another offence.[100]

The Church account book started in 1820 still exists – the last entry was made in 1971.[101] Among the recurring expenses for communion wine, washing surplices and cleaning the churchyard, there are annual payments for 'sparrows' at 3d or 6d per dozen. In 1820 there were 48 dozen at 3d and 36 dozen at 6d, in 1821 33 dozen at 3d and 17 dozen at 6d and so on until the 1840s. The total for 1826 was particularly high, when 155 dozen were recorded. There is no explanation of the difference in the price paid and it is probable that the term 'sparrows' includes other kinds of small birds; perhaps the higher price was paid for members of the crow family.

Under the Elizabethan Act of 1566 'for the Preservation of Grain' Churchwardens were required to make payments for the killing of nineteen different types of 'noyfull fowles' which were thought to compete with the human population for grain and fruit. The Act also provided for the killing of 'vermyn', although rabbits, hares and deer were exempt because they were the quarries for the gentlemen's hunting. Payments for vermin were made by the Overseers of the Poor and are therefore not recorded in the Church accounts. The Act was repealed in 1863.[102]

These payments for 'sparrows', however small, would have been a welcome addition to a family's income at a time when the average agricultural wage in Wiltshire was 7s 7d. per week, the lowest in any English county apart from Dorset. In Yorkshire it was 12s 6d because of competition for labour from the mills and factories, whilst in Wiltshire the woollen industry had declined. There were fewer jobs in the countryside due to the effects of the enclosures, the changes in farming methods and the introduction of improved tools and machinery. Britain had been fighting overseas wars since 1793 and although wages rose during that time, they fell again sharply during the agricultural depression which followed Wellington's victory at Waterloo in 1815. Conditions remained bleak for farm workers and their families, with rising prices and stagnant wages, throughout the 1830s and 1840s. It is thought that in Wiltshire about 15% of families depended on Poor Relief for their survival: the national average was 10%.

William Cobbett described his visit in 1826 to the Vale of Pewsey and the Avon Valley in his 'Rural Rides'. He contrasts the beauty and fertility of the countryside and the prosperity of the farmers with the poverty of the labourers whose work produced the abundant crops. Other commentators remarked on the slow walking pace of the Wiltshire farm workers and attributed this to the effects of malnutrition. The diet for many people was bread, with cheese if they were lucky, supplemented by potatoes grown in their gardens or on their allotments. Wiltshire meat, butter and cheese were being sold for high prices in Bath and London, making food more expensive in the county than elsewhere.

Cobbett prophesied that 'This state of affairs never can continue many years! By some means or other there must be an end to it; and my firm belief is, that the end will be dreadful.' The predicted explosion came in 1830 and though it shook the authorities, it failed to bring any immediate improvement to the condition of agricultural workers.

The introduction of threshing machines was the trigger. Threshing by hand was an indoor job which could be done in bad weather. The farm workers saw that the machines would deprive them of a major source of paid work during the winter at a time when their earnings were already at subsistence level. Trouble broke out first in Kent and spread rapidly through the southern counties, reaching Wiltshire in November 1830. Letters signed 'Captain Swing' were sent to farmers, threatening arson and the destruction of threshing machines if higher wages and better conditions were not granted. Sporadic riots and arson followed, with the hated threshing machines being especially targeted. Terrified farmers began breaking up their own machines in an attempt to avert trouble, whereupon the rioters took to demanding money.

Threshing machine of the type targeted in the riots

The following accounts of events were published in *The Devizes Gazette & Herald* of 25th November 1830 under the headline 'Lawless State of the Peasantry' – which clearly indicates where its sympathies lay.

On Friday 19th November the first disturbances occurred at Wilcot and Oare. A Pewsey correspondent reported that in Oare 'the entire stock of wheat, barley, beans and oats of Mr Fowler was destroyed by fire'. The fire engine and a contingent of men from Pewsey prevented the fire from spreading further, 'but to the utter disgrace of the peasantry of Oare, instead of rendering assistance, they appeared to be in high glee'. Pewsey men had to guard the water pipes to the fire engine, but could not prevent one pipe being cut which 'stopped the engine for a considerable time'. Some of the Oare men attempted to intimidate the Pewsey men by throwing 'brickbats' at their heads. About £400 worth of damage was done.

[The next day:] About half past eight o'clock on Saturday night, a fire was discovered on the premises of Mr Simpkins of Stanton; and almost immediately afterwards, fire issued from a barn belonging to Mr Mills of the same place. The whole of the labourers from the neighbouring farms rendered every assistance to extinguish the flames, which they ultimately subdued. But, most astonishing and unaccountable, while their exertions were applied to keep under these fires, a third was discovered in another barn, also belonging to Mr Mills, and which, with its contents, was entirely consumed. On Sunday, to gratify a lawless mob, Mr Mills, and the neighbouring farmers, felt the necessity of destroying their own threshing machines.

Other sources[103] state that in Stanton on the Saturday night two men were seen wearing 'great drab coats' and there was a third, 'a stranger, a respectably dressed man'. Mr Simpkins was at Manor Farm and Mr Mills at what is now Greywethers.

Trouble was now flaring up everywhere and the authorities reacted:

Nearly all the respectable inhabitants in the disturbed parts of the county have, since Sunday, been sworn in as Special Constables; and on Tuesday morning, four troops of the Yeomanry Cavalry assembled in Devizes, to act as occasion might require.

A threshing machine was destroyed in All Cannings. Stagecoaches were stopped at Froxfield and the passengers robbed. On Tuesday 23rd it was reported that a mob had collected in Pewsey, and another in Manningford, 'for the purpose of breaking threshing machines'. On the same day:

> A large mob assembled at Alton, where they broke two threshing machines belonging to Mr Miller and one belonging to Mr Neate; they afterwards proceeded to demolish that of Mr Robert Pile. This gentleman, however, feeling exasperated at seeing his property so wantonly destroyed, fired a pistol, and afterward a gun, loaded with large shot, in the midst of the mob, wounding two or three with the contents. The misguided men rushed immediately upon Mr Pile, and would have murdered him on the spot, but for the intervention of a labourer named Bullock, who took him in his arms, and carried him to the house.

Robert Pile had been hit on the head and his arm fractured. The mob broke into the house, smashed some of the furniture and threatened Mrs Pile (Robert's mother). She gave them £10 and they went off to Stanton and then to Woodborough. Mr Brown of Horton 'on hearing of the outrage, hastened to Devizes and communicated with the Magistrates.' The Yeomanry Cavalry, which were in readiness, followed the mob to Stanton and Woodborough. They caught up with the mob 'making merry' in a public house in Woodborough, and after a scuffle arrested 28 of them. They marched the prisoners towards Devizes but in Chirton 'a few of the scattered rabble had the temerity to attempt a rescue' and were arrested in their turn. The Yeomanry reached Devizes at about 11 pm and the prisoners were locked up in the Bridewell.

The next day, the Yeomanry 'scoured the villages of Alton, Allington, Manningford, etc.' and arrested some of the rioters, among whom was 'a fellow called Rose who has recently returned from transportation'. This did not prevent Mary Parker being robbed of a sovereign in Stanton on the following day.[104]

The *Gazette* commented that the fact that the riots had broken out so suddenly and that no one knew who was organising them 'adds a vague and mysterious kind of terror to the natural alarm which successful villany and violence must always inspire in an opulent and peaceful community.' The problem was that the 'opulence' was not shared by everyone.

The authorities began to think that perhaps the labourers' wages should be raised: the Devizes Magistrates recommended 10 shillings a week. In Kington Langley a meeting of farmers and landowners was held to discuss wage rates. 'In the meantime, the labourers, knowing the object of the meeting, met to learn the result, and when the farmers left the vestry, they were surprised to find nearly

Wiltshire horn sheep

every labourer in the parish assembled.' On being promised that their wages would be raised and the rent of their potato allotments reduced, the labourers cheered the speaker and dispersed quietly. The farmers in turn pressed the landowners to reduce their rents.

By the end of November, the disturbances had died down in Wiltshire. On 23rd December, the *Gazette* reported:

The labourers of Stanton, who promptly assisted to extinguish the fire on the premises of Mr Mills, a few weeks since, and by whose praiseworthy exertions a great part of the building were saved, had, on Tuesday last the sum of £12 10d 0d distributed amongst them; viz £5 by Mr Crockett on behalf of the Norwich Union Insurance Office; £2 10s 0d by the Mutual Insurance; and £5 was given by Lord Pembroke (the landlord). The partakers of this bounty will now be induced to contrast with delighted hearts, the humble happiness they will be enabled to enjoy in the society of their wives and children before a blazing faggot at this festive season, with the wretched, and perhaps, repentant condition of those who, awaiting in gaol the dreadful ordeal of trial, lament, too late, the infatuation which has reduced them to such misery.

Mr Crockett clearly knew how to make the most of a marketing opportunity. This announcement appeared in the same issue of the *Gazette*:

Mr Crockett begs to announce to the public that the Directors of the Norwich Union Fire Office have rescinded the order of prohibition against effecting an Insurance where a Threshing Machine is used. Mr C. will therefore be happy to receive Insurances upon those well-known liberal principles, for which this Office stands pre-eminent. A stronger proof of its liberality could not have been given, than supporting the public (at the late peculiar crisis) when most other Offices had declined continuing their protection; and it is hoped that a determination so important will meet its reward from a liberal public.

The disturbances had lasted less than a month in Wiltshire where there had been 208 incidents, the highest number in any county: 20 riots, 18 cases of arson,

62 robberies, 97 threshing machines and 4 'industrial machines' broken. In the 339 cases heard at the Special Assizes held in Salisbury in January 1831, 52 prisoners were sentenced to death (one was actually executed) and 152 to transportation; 47 were jailed and 139 bound over or acquitted.

When they came into the Court Room the prisoners saw on the Bench the landlords and farmers whose property had been attacked. Some of the farmers made pleas for clemency for individuals they knew to be of good character. This was due in some measure to a sense of justice but the thought must also have been in their minds that they would be losing a good worker to Australia and would be left with his wife and children who would then need Parish Relief.

Whilst were no overt leaders of the 'Swing' movement, agitators were clearly at work. There were some who were only interested in extorting money from householders in order to spend it in the alehouse. But the scale of the disturbances and the fact that so many usually peaceable and responsible men were taking such desperate action is a measure of the widespread and genuine distress.

11

The Stanton Diary and a New Church

M R SIMPKINS, the tenant of Little Farm, had moved into *Manor Farm House* in 1823 and the Vicar, Rev. Walter Birch, had taken over Mr Simpkin's house (now *The Old Rectory*) as the Vicarage. About two years later Rev. Birch left the village due to ill health and Rev. James Hunt Grubbe took his place as Curate.

The Rev. James was keenly interested in horticulture. In 1828 he took out Patent No. 5600 for *Grubbe's Heat-transmitting Wall for Ripening Fruit*. It was a wall made of slates fitted into frames, with trellis fixed to both sides on to which fruit trees were trained. The idea was that the slate would absorb the heat from the sun falling on the south side of the wall, and transmit it to the fruit growing on the north side, thus ripening the fruit. Unfortunately the world was not quite ready for James Hunt Grubbe's solar panel.[105]

The Rev. George Majendie became Vicar of Stanton in May 1830 but did not take up residence in the village until September 1831, having been looking after his brother Stuart during an illness. Rev. Majendie began a diary, now known as 'The Stanton Diary'. On the first page, he writes 'To my Successor'. He warns that 'in a confined sphere, trifles are apt to be invested with an undue importance' and hopes that his successor will continue the diary and faithfully preach the gospel 'to the poor people of this parish, and to do also what you can for the supply of their temporal wants.' It was a promise he himself would keep and he made an energetic start:

> The Vicarage house and premises required much alteration. I papered and painted it, changed the front, made a lawn at the back, planted shrubs and trees all round it, built a new shed in the adjoining field, and effected several other improvements.
>
> I found a large bag full of papers in the handwriting of my predecessor, who seems to have had much trouble about tithes and other temporalities. I examined these papers and burnt the greater number of them, which were of no importance. The remainder I shall leave in the Iron Chest.
>
> Shortly after my Institution, I applied to my patron, Lord Pembroke, for assistance to build two Sunday School rooms. He liberally sent me £50 which covered the whole expense.

The whirlwind of activity continued as the Vicar now set about the church.

> I found the church in a sadly dilapidated condition – the whole very damp, particularly the chancel. At my solicitation, the latter was whitewashed to remove the green stains, etc. At my own expense I removed an unsightly wooden screen which separated the chancel from the body of the church.
>
> I raised by subscription in the parish the sum of £15.4.0d to purchase a stove which is now placed in the middle of the church. To improve the Psalmody I made the singers a present of four books containing some excellent Psalm tunes which I got from my brother Henry at Sheen.

Majendie notes that according to the census return of 1831, the population of Stanton was 320. Housing conditions were poor: the 62 inhabited houses were occupied by 80 families.

The Vicar was pleased with the number of people taking communion at the Christmas service: 30 'a greater number, I believe, than at any former period'. Perhaps the stove helped. He was dismayed to find that the farmers expected their employees to work on Good Friday and that no collections were taken at the services. He was soon reflecting that the number of communicants represented only 10% of the population of the village.

In March 1832 there were two services in the church at Stanton to mark the National Fast Day on account of the outbreak of cholera which had killed 2000 people in London, the north of England and Scotland. The death toll in the cholera epidemic would eventually reach 23,000 but fortunately there were no cases in Stanton.

Meanwhile it had been decided that the old church was beyond repair and that the only thing to do was to pull it down, leaving the tower, and build a new one. Fundraising began. The imposition of a rate of 11d in the pound on the population of Stanton yielded £103 10s 10d. The Vicar himself gave £150 and the Earl of Pembroke £50. The Vicar solicited contributions from his friends and family and the clergymen of the surrounding parishes. There were six contributions from Stanton people in addition to the rate levied, including one shilling from Keziah Broomham. Just short of £500 was raised.

The diary entry for 27th May 1832 reads:

The last Sunday in the old church. Preached in the afternoon to a very full congregation on 2. Kings. 12. 11-12. Some of the old people were much affected and tearful at being in this venerable building for the last time.

28th May 1832: The work of pulling down the old church was begun very early this morning. A beautiful May morning it was. The timber of the roof, and other parts of the building, were found to be quite decayed. The walls which were about a yard in thickness were constructed of miserable stuff, very little better than rubble and road dust with hardly any lime. Nearly the whole week was occupied in pulling down and clearing away the materials.

Services for Stanton people were held at Alton Priors during the building work and the Vicar gave lectures in the school room for those unable to get to Alton.

In August the Bishop made a visitation to Devizes and held a confirmation service. The Vicar paid for two carts to take 21 Stanton people to Devizes to be confirmed and noted that four or five of those who had come forward for confirmation were middle-aged married people. Much to his annoyance, at the next communion service the Vicar found that none of the newly confirmed parishioners attended. Perhaps they thought that it was worth the trouble of being confirmed just to get a free trip to Devizes.

On 14th October, the Vicar was complaining that the church building programme was behind schedule: 'According to contract it should have been finished by the 20th September, but the roof is not yet on.' Worse was to come. On 29th October:

A very serious settlement has taken place on each side of the arch which has just been erected between the nave and chancel – caused by the great width and flatness of the arch, and the abutments on each side being on new foundations. It is fortunate that the settlement happened when it did before the completion of the building. A recurrence of the accident has been now provided against by building a pier on each side as a support to the arch, and making the arch itself higher. Plank, the builder, who has hitherto been very culpably negligent about the work, seems to have been roused by this accident and the building is now going on with far more activity.

But on 27th March 1833, the Vicar was jubilant:

This is a memorable day at Stanton. Our new church was opened for divine service, and a considerable number of the neighbouring clergy and gentry attended. I read prayers, and my brother Henry preached. The collection amounted to £32 11s 0d. I gave a cold collation to the company after the service. The next day I entertained 35 of the school children to dinner in the kitchen, and in the evening gave a supper to the clerk and singers.

The only sour note was that during the rebuilding work, someone had stolen the new church stove.

The church had been rebuilt in ten months and was a better match to the medieval tower than the old church had been. £505 had been raised, including the £32 from the collection at the inaugural service. For the Vicar, who had been in Stanton for only 18 months, it was a great achievement.

Unfortunately, as the Rev. Majendie and later vicars found, there was a price to pay for speed. As early as 1835 the Vicar was alarmed to see 'manifest symptoms of insecurity in the church walls' due, he thought, to their thinness. He had four strong buttresses built by White of Devizes at a cost of £50, to which the Vestry contributed one third. At the same time, repairs were carried out to the porch and battlements which had been badly built.

For the moment though, the mood was joyful:

May 26th Whitsunday. There was an interesting scene in our new church. Ten children, born during the rebuilding and privately baptised, were in the middle of the afternoon service admitted into the church. The children and their sponsors filled almost the whole chancel.

At he beginning of 1832 the Vicar set up a Coal Club and two Clothing Clubs, one for children's clothes and the other for adults. Members contributed twopence a week to the Clothing Clubs and a penny a week for coal during the year. £27 1s 11d was collected for the Clothing Clubs and £7 7s 4d for the Coal Club. To this were added donations from the Vicar, the Earl of Pembroke and others. A total of £51 worth of clothing and bedding was purchased and members collected their orders from the schoolroom around Christmas time. £14 14s 8d worth of coal was delivered to members' homes. Two years later, Clothing Club members received vouchers to spend at a shop in Devizes, which they preferred. (It is interesting that it was obviously not difficult to get to Devizes.) This proved popular and similar clubs were still running in Stanton well into the 20th century.

The schoolroom was probably in the Vicarage grounds because in 1834 the Vicar paid for a large bell to be put up on 'the roof of the scullery'. It was to be used twice a day to summon the children to school and to be rung in case of fire or other alarms at night. An educational enquiry in 1833 states that the school had been enlarged the previous year, presumably meaning the two new 'Sunday School rooms' for which Lord Pembroke had paid. Daily attendance varied between 20 and 45 children, depending on the demands of farm work. Parents paid a penny a week for each child with the Vicar subsidising the running costs of the school.

There had been a school in Stanton since before 1818. In that year a report to the Select Committee on the Education of the Poor recorded that 20 poor children went to the day school. In addition, two separate Sunday schools for girls and boys were attended by a total of 62 children. At a time when there was no official 'school leaving age' there was pressure on the children of poorer families to leave school at an early age and begin contributing to the family income. For this reason many Sunday Schools gave lessons in reading and writing, as well as religious instruction.

The Vicar in 1835 was trying a social experiment:

A little before Easter, April 12th, I opened a writing school for young men on Sabbath Evenings. The young men, between 16 and 25 years of age, are generally an idle and unruly set and in a country parish they generally are particularly noisy and vicious on Sabbath Evenings. With the view of keeping them out of mischief, and bringing them within the reach of better influences, I have prevailed upon 18 or 20 of them to meet for two or three hours every Sunday evening to write copies of Scripture texts and words, and while they write to listen to the reading of some good book. I generally attend myself for about an hour for the purpose of reading to them. The effect has been most evident, immediately, in tranquillising the village and I hope that much good will result from the experiment. The old school master William Rabbets instructs them in writing and his house serves as the schoolroom. I pay a penny a head and the scholars a halfpenny each.

The Diary records in November that this Sunday evening class for young men continued to be well attended and 'to answer the purpose for which I formed it'. The Vicar had also been giving lectures for adults on Wednesday evenings, sometimes in his own kitchen if the weather was cold. They had been popular but were discontinued in the spring and summer because people needed to work on their potato allotments.

In April 1833 the Vicar and the Churchwardens, Mr Simpkins and Mr Hitchcock, appeared before the Charity Commissioners at the *Bear Hotel* in Devizes to give an account of the Fowle & Smith Charity. At the meeting the Vicar had something to say:

I informed the Commissioners that the produce of the land, amounting to about £16, had this year been given by the Trustees to persons emigrating to America, instead of being applied, as it should have been, to apprentice some poor child. The Churchwardens were obliged to plead guilty to this misappropriation of the money and promised that nothing of the kind should occur again.

The account book which begins in 1820,[106] and which was almost certainly produced at this meeting, shows that £30 12s 5d had been 'paid for Emigrants to America' plus £2 13s 8d in April 1832 to D Harvey for 'carriage to Poole'. Before that entry, the book records a number of payments for apprenticing both boys and girls.

The Charity Commissioners' Report dated 10th January 1834 bears out the Vicar's account of the meeting and states that 'the parish intended in future to apply the whole of the rents received from the charity land in putting out apprentices.' The Commissioners approved of the land being let out as allotments to the poor, which had been done since 1829, particularly as it brought in a higher return at that time (about £15 from which £2 to £3 was deducted for tithes and taxes).

Questions were asked about the whereabouts of the previous account book, thought to contain 'the only authentic account of the above charity, and many other things interesting to the parish of Stanton'. It had last been seen in the possession of Mr Simpkins, who said he 'knew not what had become of it'. The Vicar strongly suspected that the book had been 'purposely destroyed'. He was keen to obtain accurate information about the intentions of the charity's donor and searched in vain for his Will in the Registrar's office in Salisbury.[107]

Emigration to America or Canada (sometimes described as 'British America') was seen as a way of escaping the low wages and poor prospects in English agriculture. Seductive advertisements appeared in the newspapers, promising fertile land for purchase or rent, 'English laws and customs' but no game laws and no taxes except 2s per 100 acres. This appealed to smallholders who were struggling to make a living. Emigration was also advocated by some as a means of getting rid of the surplus population of 'paupers'.

At about half past five on 29th October 1833 John Hams of Stanton was coming home from Devizes where he had collected his army pension. It was beginning to get dark and he had only a short distance to go to Stanton when William Rose jumped out at him from behind a haystack and knocked him down. Rose struck John Hams several violent blows to his face and head and robbed him of £3 10s 6d. John Hams recognised his assailant. The constable who arrested William Rose stated that there was blood on his jacket. William Rose was found guilty and sentenced to death, whereupon he protested his innocence loudly. The Judge then said that Rose had only recently returned from transportation, which did not appear to have had a salutary effect on him and that if his life were spared, this time he would be transported for life.[108] It is probable that this was the same Rose who was arrested during the Swing riots.

In 1834 the Vicar let some glebe land as four allotments for farm workers to grow potatoes. He notes with satisfaction that the new 'Beer bill' for licensing alehouses had come into effect and that Mr Broomham, who brewed and sold beer on his premises in Stanton – 'and much drunkenness and revelry was the consequence' – had not been granted a licence.

The weather in 1835 was extreme, a very cold winter followed by a long hot summer. In Stanton, the farm workers were saying that they could not remember such an abundant crop of wheat, calling it a 'double crop'. Wages in Stanton were down to six shillings a week for labourers. In this year, the new Poor Law came into effect. The system of Parish Relief given to people in their own homes was to be discontinued and paupers were to be sent to Work Houses where conditions were intentionally made as unpleasant as possible. A Work House was to be built for each 'Union' which covered a number of villages. Stanton was to be in the Devizes Union.

A notebook used by one of Lord Pembroke's Agents exists.[109] He did not write his name in it, so his identity is not certain. The majority of entries are the statistics he needed for his work, but he bursts out passionately about the regime proposed for the Work Houses:

> The separation of husband from wife – mother from children – brother from sister, which is to be carried into effect in this Establishment, appears tyrannical and fraught with danger. I doubt if the poor people will submit to it with patience. I hear some old folks who have been most respectable in their day, and who have of late been supported in their own cottages by the Parish – all these will be forced into the workhouse as outdoor relief will absolutely cease. All this may be politic – it is at all events the refinement of cruelty, as it appears to me.

The new system treated poverty as a crime. Dread of this shame and degradation was still attached to former work house buildings in older people's minds until the end of the 20th century.

In his book the Agent notes a 'terrible' fall in prices for agricultural produce in 1835. Wheat was selling at £9 per load compared to £26 in the previous year. The Estate's tenants were despondent and many were in arrears with their rent. Two hundred people were out of work in Wilton out of a population of less than 2000. Lady Pembroke was providing employment by improving the grounds of Wilton House.

In Stanton the Vicar was improving the look of the churchyard. He planted trees and shrubs on the north side of the churchyard and fenced it with iron railings. He persuaded Mr Hitchcock to pull down an 'ugly mud wall' and an unsightly old barn and this had 'improved the appearance of the village, as seen from the Devizes road'. Mr Hitchcock had been allowed to make the path across the churchyard from the door in the Church Farm wall to the chancel, which still exists.

The Diary contains notes about local events: the death of Rev. Augustus Hare, the eminent and well-liked vicar of Alton Barnes whom Rev. Majendie counts as a friend, the Vicar's interest in the Church Missionary Society and the opening on 15th August 1835 of the new Assize Court in Devizes, which had been financed by public subscription. The Vicar was particularly incensed about the Rev. Philpot, who had joined the nonconformists and was preaching at Allington.

The Rev. Majendie spent a lot of money in the village: £150 towards the cost of building the church, plus the various repairs to the tower and remedial work necessary due to the poor construction of the nave and chancel. He had paid for repairs and renovation to the Vicarage and for improving the garden there and the churchyard. Responding to an official enquiry into the Revenue of Ecclesiastical Benefices, he calculated that the net income of the living was £221 9s 6d, and anticipated that it would be less in future because he had signed a 12 year agreement 'with the principal Farmer' to receive 10% less in tithes because of the general economic situation. His income came from renting out the glebe land and from tithes. His annual outgoings included £10 for the Sunday School and about £20 for the Clothing and Coal Clubs. He complained that 'the farmers give nothing' and that there is 'no gentleman in the place'.

Towards the end of 1835 the Vicar comments that his health is not good and consequently he has stopped the Wednesday evening lectures that winter. There are few entries for the following year, and after October 1836 the diary falls silent. In 1839 the Rev. Majendie resigned the living of Stanton in favour of his brother-in-law, Rev. George Thompson Ward and went to Heddington, where he died in 1842, aged 47.

The Rev. Ward took up residence in Stanton on 2nd October 1839 and in the tradition of new vicars, immediately redecorated the Vicarage. He continued his predecessor's routine, including the Wednesday lecture and the diary. On 13th December he had a 'handsome stove' installed in the church, which was very welcome after the theft of the previous one.

The clubs had been amalgamated into one Clothing and Coal Club and he notes that only labourers were eligible to join; tradesmen were not. Rev. Ward seems to have established better relations with the farmers who, he says, have 'very liberally stepped forward to help me in sustaining the club and the school'. Mary Ann Powell received a salary of £10 a year as Governess of the School. Children paid one penny a week to attend the school.

Blacksmith's shop - Mr Tasker moved to this site in 1840, probably to this building

There is the first mention of medical care. On 26th May the Vicar sent 'my poor parishioner Susan Maslen to Bath Hospital'. She returned on 10th October 'not much better'. Ann Buckland who had cataracts also went, but the outcome is not recorded in her case.

In November 1840 the Vicar improved the entrance to the Vicarage by negotiating with Mr Tasker to move the blacksmiths and carpenters shops. This involved some exchanges of strips of land and the payment of £25 to Mr Tasker to move the forge. Together with improvements to the Vicarage orchard, this cost the Vicar £40 which he could only just afford. He felt this expenditure was justified because it achieved the removal of the forge, a constant source of 'Noise, Smoke and Dirt'. He states that 'The old path ran in a straight line from the kitchen door to Mr

Artist's impression of the interior of the blacksmith's shop. The leather bellows are in storage in Stanton

Tasker's stable, in the midst of many nuisances which were intolerable to a lady (my sister resided with me at this time).' The Rev. Majendie had previously paid for a rough stone bridge to replace the slippery stepping stones across the winterbourne.

The year ends with a note that Philip Harvey had died of 'the fever which has killed many in the neighbourhood'. Stanton was spared an epidemic due, in the Vicar's opinion, to the 'liberal use of the chloride of lime in water sprinkled about. It is a most efficacious preventive against contagion'. After 1840 Rev. Ward made no further entries in the diary.

12

A Chapel, New Houses and Two Fires

S INCE 1810 the possibility of transporting heavy goods and raw materials relatively cheaply on the canal had been changing the appearance of the area and opening up possibilities for industry and employment. Roofing slates, brick and stone became affordable for more modest buildings, coal transformed domestic life, grain and non-perishable agricultural products could be traded further afield.

In 1812 Samuel Robbins moved his timber business from Pewsey to Honey Street, where over the years an industrial complex developed. To meet the needs of the growing transport business on the canals and rivers, he began to build boats, including trows, the sailing barges used on the River Severn. Eventually the company diversified into related products, making tarpaulins, wagon cloths, tar oil and colours. An important part of the business was the trade in coal and slate and the transport of heavy goods.[110] Honey Street offered good employment possibilities for Stanton people.

Other enterprises grew up on the canal. John Clarke was a Coal, Slate and Salt merchant with depots at the wharves in Devizes and Burbage who found *Stanton House* a convenient place to live. His letterhead states that he also traded 'in building and paving bricks, Newbury gravel, hurdles, etc.' There is a note in small print: 'N.B. A Market Boat leaves Burbage Wharf every Wednesday, at One o'Clock, and takes in Corn at all intermediate places for Devizes Market.'[111]

In 1841 John Clarke built a Methodist Chapel in the village on the path to *The Mansion*, just past *Forge Cottage* and *Rookery Nook*. In its heyday the chapel was in the midst of the forge and its outbuildings but fortunately Sunday was a day of rest. The chapel could seat 100 and attendances were said to average 60 people in 1850-1,[112] probably coming from the neighbouring villages as well as from Stanton. Because it was closed in 1913, information on the chapel is scant. A rare survival is the receipt book for 1901 for the Stanton Sunday School which lists payments of one shilling each from 23 children, eight of them living in Stanton.

From the Circuit Books for the Devizes area it seems that very few Stanton people were counted as 'members' in the sense of paying a subscription to the Circuit, although obviously many more attended the services. In 1837 there are 7 members and 9 in 1839. There were 10 at Lady Day in 1840, but only 8 by midsummer, two people being described as 'backsliders'. Thereafter there were 3 or 4 members each year, with a surge to 10 in 1855 and back to 4 in the following year but with '14 believers'. Collections were made for the splendidly named 'Worn-out Ministers' and Widows' Auxiliary Fund'.

John Clarke was of course the first Steward of the Stanton Chapel. He was succeeded after his death in 1849 by Thomas Hailstone who held the position for many years and remained Steward of the Alton and Stanton chapels after they were combined in 1861. There was a strong following for Methodism in Honey Street, and Thomas Pinniger and Edward Lane appear on the list of Trustees of the chapel.

Many reasons are given for the rise of nonconformity, but one is without a doubt the power which the landholders and the Church of England had over the lives of working people in the villages. Landholders controlled jobs, wage rates and housing, acted as Churchwardens and in other local government roles, served on juries, administered the law as magistrates, made the law as Members of Parliament and were the only people entitled to vote. Apart from the alehouse, the chapel or meeting house was the only place where working people could have a voice.

In the election for the MP for Wiltshire in 1819 there were only two voters in Stanton: Isaac Simpkins as a freeholder and Stephen Tasker as a freeholder and Parish Clerk. The Reform Act of 1832 relaxed the property qualification to include leaseholders and copyholders with a rental of at least £50 per annum. In 1833 there were five Stanton men on the electoral roll and by 1842 there were 10: Thomas Broomham, John Fowle, Daniel Fowle, Simon Hitchcock, Henry Mills, John Simpkins, Adam Maslen, Rev. J Thompson Ward and the holders of the mills, Michael Tasker and Thomas Page.[113] The Reform Act of 1869 extended the franchise to occupants of land valued at £12, and by the end of the century 48 men had the vote in Stanton.

Changes were also taking place in the ancient system of funding the Church of England. Since medieval times parish priests had held glebe land which they either farmed themselves or, more commonly, let for rent. In addition they were entitled to receive tithes: one tenth of the agricultural produce of the village each year: grain, fruit, honey, eggs, hay and wood. This included the increase of farm stock: one in ten of the animals born. By the 19th century, most clergy were receiving their tithes in cash rather than in kind. During the agricultural depression in the 1820s and 1830s, it was felt, not least by the clergy themselves, that it was time to reform this archaic system. The Tithe Commutation Act of 1836 appointed Tithe Commissioners and provided for a survey to be carried out in each parish to determine the liability for tithes of each landholder and then to agree an annual Rent Charge to be paid instead, based on the prices of wheat, barley and oats.

Stanton was found to contain 1980 acres of land 'by estimation': 1031 acres of arable, 918 acres of meadow, 3 acres of woodland and 28 acres of 'homesteads, gardens and orchards.' On 18th April 1844 an agreement was reached to pay a total of £570 – £170 to the Vicar and £400 to the Earl of Pembroke who was the lessee of the Prebendary. Of the farmers, John Simpkins and Simon Hitchcock both paid £55, Henry Mills £29 and Daniel Fowle £6 15s 6d. There were other smaller payments, including John Clarke who paid 7s 6d. Three copies of the Tithe Map were made, one of which is still kept in the village.

Lord Pembroke's Agent was still keeping his notebook until 1840 when he left Wilton. The audits of the receipts of the Estate were held twice a year over three days in June and December. The principal tenants attended the audit and were entertained to dinner. Stanton tenants paid their rents in July and February. In 1839 the rents received by the Earl from the whole of his Estate were £10,918 and in November £12,073 – 'the largest of modern times'.

The Agent records wheat prices which fell to their lowest in 1835 then rose steadily. There were natural disasters. In 1837 'the backward season has caused the death of many sheep from actual starvation'. There was cattle murrain in 1840, 'many lost their hooves and thousands at Weyhill Fair were diseased'. Again in 1837 'the destruction caused by the hurricane last November was frightful. Numerous trees of very large size were blown down and still lie in the Park (at Wilton) not being available at present to use. The timber yard is full of wood. Much damage was also occasioned to the buildings of the tenants which will make their allowances for repairs somewhat serious.'

The state of housing was causing concern; cottages were in a 'ruinous state'. The Estate had not been responsible for the repair or replacement of buildings when tenancies were 'for lives' and tenants were either unwilling or unable to invest money in buildings which they did not own. Most tenancies were now held on an annual rent with the responsibility for paying for repairs being negotiated between the Estate and the tenant. Tenants were generally given an allowance of half the cost of bricks and other materials, with two thirds being allowed for very old buildings.

With some prosperity returning to agriculture, the Pembroke Estate instructed Cyrus Combes to produce a survey and map of Stanton, partly with a view to improving its buildings. The result was a beautiful and detailed map dated 1853, which together with the 1851 census, gives an insight into the changes that had taken place since the Enclosure survey of 1784.

The most obvious change was that the two largest farms had grown in size to about 900 acres each, and were called 'East Farm' and 'West Farm'. East Farm had developed from Isaac Simpkin's holding of 197 acres known in 1784 as 'Little Farm'. His descendent and successor John Simpkins now lived at *Manor Farm House*. The former 'Great Farm' of 785 acres was now West Farm held by Henry Hitchcock who lived in *Church Farm House*.

Comparing the maps of 1874 and 1853, the fate of the smaller farms is evident. The houses and outbuildings opposite Manor Farm House had completely disappeared, including the extensive premises of Thomas Dykes who in 1784 farmed 106 acres. John Godwin's house and barns (on the site of *The Row*) had gone. Mr Mills had left *Greywethers* which was now occupied by Mrs Crowther and was no longer a farmhouse. The barns and outbuildings along Calf Lane had disappeared leaving only some of the houses. The forge, the Methodist chapel and the house now called *The Mansion* had been built on a former smallholding.

There were now two inns in the parish: The Barge on the canal and a less imposing establishment on the site of *Lydnarda*, where Jane Fowle described herself as a grocer and beer retailer. The field between the canal and *Stanton House* was let out to farm workers by the Pembroke Estate as 'garden allotments', part of the 15 acres which the Estate allocated to 'the poor'.

The 1851 census recorded a population of 349 living in 71 houses, with 5 houses uninhabited. Henry Hitchcock employed 45 labourers, a cook, a housemaid, a dairymaid and a groom. John Simpkins' workforce was 'about 40' and he had two servants. John Harvey described himself as a 'farmer of 7 acres'. William Clarke, son of John Clarke who founded the chapel, was a coal merchant and also farmed

26 acres (leased from Daniel Fowle) employing four men and six boys. Fifty-one men and fifteen women were listed as 'agricultural labourers', with ten carters, seven shepherds, two woodmen and fourteen ploughboys – a total of 99 people.

Of the craftsmen, three men worked for Michael Tasker in his blacksmith's shop and two men on his 28-acre farm. Two master carpenters each employed one journeyman and one apprentice: John Powell (on the site of 1 and 2 Hillview) and Charles Crook. There were two master shoemakers and two journeymen. Other craftsmen included a thatcher, a master bricklayer, a harness maker, a basket maker and a washerwoman. A cooper's apprentice and a journeyman tailor may have worked outside the village. There were another four servants. The wife of a private soldier also lived in the village.

The Wharf at Honey Street was providing employment for a sail-maker, two sawyers, a 'navigator' and possibly others. Thomas Chandler at The Barge employed one man. Two boatmen and one boatman's wife are evidence of the importance of canal transport.

Charles Bromham and Jane Tasker were the schoolteachers for the 33 children listed as 'scholars'. The new school (now the Village Hall) had been built next to the churchyard in 1849, partly at the expense of the Vicar, Rev. Thompson Ward.

Seventeen people were described as 'paupers', mostly elderly, with a former groom being 'relieved from the Marlborough Club'.

Only one mill remained in operation, Stoniford Mill which, confusingly, was now becoming known as Stanton Mill. The miller was Isaac Berry who employed one man. In the early 19th century, technical developments were making watermills more efficient and it was possible to bring in new machinery on the canal. At the same time there was increasing use of watermeadows. The lower mill was now

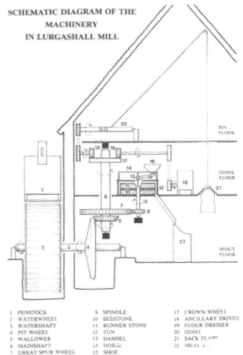

SCHEMATIC DIAGRAM OF THE MACHINERY IN LURGASHALL MILL

1 PENSTOCK	9 SPINDLE	17 CROWN WHEEL
2 WATERWHEEL	10 BEDSTONE	18 ANCILLARY DRIVES
3 WATERSHAFT	11 RUNNER STONE	19 FLOUR DRESSER
4 PIT WHEEL	12 TUN	20 HOIST
5 WALLOWER	13 DAMSEL	21 SACK FLAP
6 MAINSHAFT	14 HORSE	22 MEAL &
7 GREAT SPUR WHEEL	15 SHOE	
8 STONE NUT	16 GRAIN HOPPER	

The workings of a 19th century watermill. Courtesy of the Weald and Downland Museum, Singleton

part of East Farm and after a dispute about taking water from the millstream for flooding watermeadows, Mr Simpkins had converted the former Stanton Mill to a dairy farm. This became known as Stanton Dairy.

In 1840 one of the last roads in England to be turnpiked was the Kennett to Amesbury road, which starts at West Kennett on the London to Bath road, crosses the downs at Knap Hill and continues southwards through Alton Barnes to just north of Amesbury. This was done by an Act of Parliament, setting up a turnpike trust which kept the road in good repair and maintained bridges and causeways, financing the work by charging tolls. The network of turnpiked roads which had been developing over the previous century had speeded up the transport of goods and people. The new turnpike was of great benefit to Samuel Robbins, whose business at Honey Street was flourishing.

However, the canal was soon to face competition from the railways. In 1838, Lord Pembroke's Agent had made an entry in his notebook:

> November 29th 1838. My first journey by a railroad. The engine could not make much head against the wind which was furious and the Train was delayed upon the road for three hours. I did not reach Salisbury until 11 at night instead of 6.

Rail travel improved after that, although for some years third class passengers travelled in open carriages with wooden bench seats. In 1841 the Great Western Railway completed its broad gauge line from London to Bristol. By 1852 the GWR had taken over the Kennet & Avon Canal Company and the canal faced a slow decline. Samuel Robbins fought back. Realising that he needed to bring in more expertise, in 1860 he formed Robbins, Lane & Pinniger Limited. The company still operated a fleet of canal boats and its range of activities had expanded still further to include the production of artificial manures (using animal carcases) and super phosphate of lime. The GWR refused to carry the sulphuric acid needed for the manufacture of the artificial manure so the carboys were transported by canal.

In 1858 a serious fire at The Barge Inn destroyed nearly the whole building. The cellars were looted, resulting in 'drunkenness and confusion'. The Barge was an important provisioning point for canal boats and was rebuilt in six months under the direction of Ben Biggs of Robbins & Co.

Competition from the railway came even closer in 1862 with the opening of a singletrack broad gauge line from Bedwyn to Devizes . The GWR operated the line on behalf of the owners, the Berks. and Hants. Extension Railway. The track crossed the southern tip of the parish of Stanton and severed the path to Beechingstoke. There were stations at Savernake, Pewsey and Woodborough. This opened up new opportunities for the farmers in Stanton, because churns of fresh milk could be taken to Woodborough Station by horse and cart and transported to London.

By 1859 the church again needed major repairs[114]. The arch between the nave and chancel was rebuilt, the chancel roof was strengthened and general restoration work was carried out to the inside of the building. New pews were installed to seat 164, forty of them under the gallery for the school and Sunday school children, boys and girls on opposite sides of the aisle. Twenty-five 'free and unappropriated' seats were provided. The remaining pews were rented to members of the congregation, the wealthier households also paying for seats at the back of the church for their servants. There was seating in the chancel for the choir and an organ was installed. Thereafter the church account books list annual payments to an 'organ blower'. (The organ was moved in 1896 into the room now used as the vestry). The work cost £150, of which £130 was raised by subscription.

In May 1859 the *Devizes Advertiser* reported a gift to Stanton:

> The poor people of this village have recently been the recipients of a £50 legacy under the will of the late Mr Jas Sherry of Upavon and formerly of this parish. It has been according to the requirements of the will equitably distributed amongst the poor in amounts varying from 12s to 17s 6d by the Rev G T Ward, the Vicar and Henry Hitchcock Esq., churchwarden. We understand that some other places have been similarly favoured by this eccentric but good old man.

Wages for farm labourers in Wiltshire were 7s or 8s a week at this time.

The 12th Earl of Pembroke died in 1862 and was succeeded by his nephew who was 12 years old. During the new Earl's minority the Estate was overseen by a committee which met twice a year until 1871.[115] Mr Robson, the Agent, reported to this committee but the minute book does not record the names of its members. The impression is that the management of the Estate was humane. The Agent brought to the committee cases of hardship among families who had lived on the Estate for many years (none from Stanton). There were instances of annuities being granted to the widows or unmarried daughters of deceased tenants and of rent arrears being remitted. Concern was expressed about the poor state of the farm workers' housing. The 'Great Western Railway Fund', presumably the rent paid by the GWR for its tracks on Estate land, was used to finance new houses in several villages.

A house at Church Walk – one of two pairs built by the Earl of Pembroke's trustees, completed in 1863

The new houses being built in Stanton were pencilled in on the 1853 map. The two pairs of houses in Church Walk were completed and occupied by June 1863 and the six houses in *The Row* by the autumn of 1867, all financed from 'Railway money'. The houses were built by Estate labour and *The Row* took three years to build. The old cottages from which the tenants had moved were pulled down. There is a mystery about a pair of houses which have been pencilled in on the map in Calf Lane but which were not built.

In June 1862 the Vicar, Rev. Ward asked for a contribution towards the £19. 2s 8d he had paid for repairs to the schoolroom, but no assistance was forthcoming. The Vicar pointed out that the Schoolmistress lived in his house and that he provided her with board and lodging and paid one third of her salary. He asked whether a sitting room and bedroom could be built on to one of the new cottages for the use of the Schoolmistress. It was noted that Lord Pembroke paid £10 to the school, £10 for coal and £12 to the Clothing Club each year.

Relations with the farmers were not always smooth. Mr Hitchcock was complaining that his rent was too high and an independent valuation had to be obtained. Mr Simpkins' heart was not in his job. Mr Robson repeatedly remonstrated with him about his 'bad farming' and his land being 'foul'. Mr Simpkins threatened to give up the farm and then wrote to say he had no intention of doing so. In June 1869 the Agent reported that:

> Mr Simpkins a short time ago came to Wilton with his second son and informed Mr Robson that the Son was engaged to a Lady of large property in London and that the marriage would take place if the Son were accepted as Tenant of the Farm which he was willing to give up to him.
>
> The Son has been brought up as a Farmer and is likely, especially if he has command of capital, to prove a better Tenant than the Father of whose system of management Mr Robson latterly has been compelled to complain.

One of the committee members commented, 'I should make sure of the Lady first'. However, at the next meeting it was reported that Mr Simpkins had been succeeded in the Farm by his son, who was now married, and that repairs costing £90 had been made to the house.

An entry in December 1870 is an echo from another time:

> A copyhold estate of 24 acres fell in hand by the death of Mr Fowle in America on 26th November 1869. A heriot of the best beast then became due but does not seem to be obtainable.

The committee ceased to meet after June 1871 when the Earl came of age.

Although economic conditions had improved since the 1840s, wages remained very low. In sickness or old age people had to rely on their families or perhaps a sympathetic employer, otherwise the Work House in Devizes loomed. Between 1866 and 1902 eight Stanton people ended their days there. People found other ways to provide themselves with some security. The Wiltshire Friendly Society was formed in 1828 and is still in existence. In the 19th century the Society offered several types of insurance: for sickness, old age, childbirth, children and death. Local stewards were responsible for collecting the monthly subscriptions and paying out benefits. The Society organised social events. The *Devizes Advertiser* of 7th June 1860 reports on a Wiltshire Friendly Society meeting:

> The Stanton branch of this Society held their customary anniversary on Wednesday week and the weather proving fine the meeting was a great success. In the morning, before church time, the club paid a visit to All Cannings, and returned to Stanton church, where an excellent sermon was delivered by the Reverend F Methuen, after which a most substantial dinner was partaken of by the club, towards which the neighbouring gentry subscribed with their accustomed liberality.
>
> The evening was most pleasantly spent on the beautiful lawn in front of the Rectory which, thanks to the Rector, the Reverend E T Ward, was thrown open to them, when for 3 or 4 hours a large portion of the company danced on the green sward to the strains of an excellent band which was in attendance. The meeting broke up early, and the members dispersed to their homes, apparently thoroughly tired as well as highly delighted with their day's amusement.

Also in 1860, the St Bernard's Club issued a printed rulebook [116] with a dramatic alpine rescue scene on the cover, complete with two St Bernard dogs equipped with barrels. The club met four times a year at The Barge Inn, and was open to applicants in good health aged between 18 and 37, those older paying an extra premium. The ostensible purpose of the club was to provide insurance in case of sickness, unless the member had brought the condition upon himself by an 'act of bravado' including 'fighting, leaping, race-running or during a state of intoxication'. The impression is that it was a thinly disguised drinking club.

The Stanton inn, known as The Wheatsheaf, came to a dramatic end. Charles Deadman and his wife Dinah sold groceries at the inn, brewed beer and Charles made barrels. Charles died in July 1876, leaving a Will naming his wife and William Hailstone as executors, but Dinah also died three months later[117]. All their children were still under 21. Ann, their eldest daughter, married Maurice Fidler in February 1877. The couple

Cover of the rulebook of the St Bernard's Club

took over the inn in defiance of the executor before the estate had been formally wound up and ran up huge bills from local suppliers. Various lawsuits ensued. Finally, the court ordered the inn and its contents to be sold to pay the debts and large legal fees, and a bailiff was sent to guard the property. The *Devizes & Wiltshire Gazette* of 11th April 1878 carried the following report:

> Fire at Stanton St Bernard – About 12 at noon on Monday last, a man named Thomas Amor, who had been put in charge, as bailiff, of the house and goods and chattels of the late Mr Charles Deadman, brewer, at Stanton, was sitting by the fire when he noticed some burning particles fall from the chimney. He looked up it, and seeing a mass of fire, about as big as the crown of his hat, he ran outside, and there saw a quantity of smoke issuing from the chimney. Almost immediately afterwards flames burst through the thatch, and an alarm having been raised, Mr Pinniger despatched a messenger to Devizes for the fire engines, while a telegraphic message was sent to Pewsey with the same object.

The engines from both towns were sent as soon as possible; but by the time they arrived, the fire had got such complete hold on Deadman's house that it was burnt to the ground, and all the efforts that were used were unavailing to save five cottages adjoining, as well as a cottage on the opposite side of the road belonging to Mr Pinniger. The greater part of the furniture was saved; but Deadman's daughter, who happened to be in a neighbour's cottage at the time, lost the whole of her clothing, and had neither a hat nor a bonnet left to wear.

Amor was acting as bailiff for Mr Neate, the auctioneer, of Pewsey, and a sale of Deadman's furniture and house was to have taken place in the course of a few days. Deadman's house and Mr Pinniger's cottage were, we understand, insured. Mr Taylor, the Vicar, and the leading inhabitants rendered assistance: and a subscription has, we hear, since been set on foot for the relief of the inmates of the cottages. In one of them there were eight children.

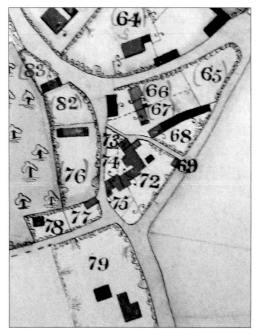

Site of the inn (no.72) and houses burned down. Thomas Pinniger's house is no. 79 (from the 1853 Estate map)

Another account in the *Devizes & Wilts Advertiser* states that the wind was very strong and that the other neighbouring cottages were saved because wet sheets were spread over their thatch. The fire engine from Honey Street was also brought but could not get enough water. Thomas Pinniger took charge and had the goods which could be saved from the houses taken into his yard at *Stanton House*. These included two horses, a wagon, a cart and a chaffcutter as well as some furniture and clocks. The telegraph must have been at Robbins, Lane & Pinniger at Honey Street Wharf as the post office at Alton Barnes was too small to have one at this date.

Tired though he was from these exertions, Thomas Pinniger had had enough of the rowdy inn and seized the opportunity to prevent it being rebuilt. Later in the day of the fire, 8th April 1878, he wrote to the solicitors dealing with Charles Deadman's estate, offering to buy the land 'at valuation' and his offer was accepted. The insurance company paid £320 to Deadman's estate for the inn.

13

Better Times

AGRICULTURE again faced a slump in the 1870s due to the importing of American grain, and in the census of 1871 several people are recorded as 'out of employ'. Seven men had smallholdings of between 3 and 9 acres, in addition to their other trades. There was one farmer of 30 acres employing one man, whilst Mr Hitchcock and Mr Simpkins each employed about 45 people: men, women and boys. Stanton was fortunate that the railway made the dairy industry possible, ensuring a reasonable standard of living.

There were changes: some familiar faces disappeared and new ones arrived. In about 1873 James Tayler and his mother, born Caroline Hitchcock, moved into what is now *Church Farm House* and took over Great Farm from Henry Hitchcock. After 38 years' service to Stanton, the Rev. Ward was succeeded in 1877 by Rev. Powell, who stayed until 1882 when the Rev. Dixon-Stewart took over the parish.

From the 1870s until the 1920s the *North Wiltshire Church Magazine* is a source of information about life in Stanton. The social activities centred on the church are recorded: Christmas and Easter celebrations, Harvest suppers, choir outings, flower shows and garden parties. It is the chronicle of a lively community, self-sufficient, well-ordered and hierarchical, but revealing now and again the hardships of daily life.

The magazine also reports on the school. Legislation, beginning with the Elementary Education Act of 1870, made education compulsory, raised the school leaving age to 13 and brought schools under the supervision of the County Council. For forty-five years, the Stanton school had been supported consistently by the

Rev. Majendie followed by Rev. Ward, and the school building met the criteria set out in the 1870 Act. The school was thereafter regularly inspected both by the Diocesan and the government inspectors. In 1876, the Diocesan Inspector reported:

Bell on the school building

> Knowledge of the Old Testament and Scripture excellent of the first division. Religious knowledge good. Repetition good. Discipline and tone good. The knowledge of the children shows that great care has been expended on their teaching. The upper classes are better in proportion to the lower.

In 1893 the government inspector stated:

> The children are orderly and making good progress in the elementary subjects. The boys show a good knowledge of geography and the girls do their needlework very nicely. The infants are making fair progress.

Among the dedicated Stanton teachers was Charles Broomham, who taught at the school for over 30 years from 1848.

There was a flourishing Sunday School, which in the 1880s numbered between 65 and 70 children. A photograph exists, taken outside the church some time in the late 1890s, showing a group of healthy children dressed in their Sunday best with their teachers, most of whom were young ladies from the better-off families in the village. Treats were organised for the children, as reported in the *Church Magazine* in 1885:

> On Thursday 24th September, the Vicar gave his annual treat to the Sunday school children, numbering nearly 70. They assembled in the church for a short service and address, and after walking in procession with their teachers to the vicarage, engaged in cricket and various games. A substantial meal of tea, cake and bread-and-butter followed, and at 6 all repaired to the school where the mothers of some of the children also assembled to witness the prize giving by Mrs Dixon-Stewart of articles of clothing, for regularity and good conduct. Miss Pinniger also gave her younger classes pretty and useful prizes. Miss Tayler and the Messrs. Tayler

and Miss B Pinniger and Mr Lewis Pinniger kindly gave up their afternoon to amusing their Sunday scholars.

The village celebrated Christmas with enthusiasm. The church was always decorated and services were well attended. Carols were sung round the village and the money collected paid for a supper for the men of the choir and a tea for the choirboys.

In the summer the annual flower show was held in the Vicarage grounds. In 1885 it was a glorious summer day:

> Great numbers of villagers and neighbours came together to spend an enjoyable afternoon. A very substantial tea was provided for all comers at 6d per head by Mr Marshall. Some capital tugs of war were organised by the Vicar, and as the afternoon wore on the scene was enlivened by dancing to the strains of the Beechingstoke Band, which played with great spirit.
>
> Mr Burt of Devizes was present with a good assortment of ironmongery. At 6 pm the lucky prize-winners assembled to receive their prizes from Mrs Dixon-Stewart, having previously made their choice of useful or ornamental articles; one bonny little girl marching off in great triumph with her own special choice of a large black saucepan – she having won a prize for a pretty wild flower nosegay.

The list of 24 adult winners is given in full; classes included vegetables of all kinds, blackcurrants, honey and 'window plants' with 10 children winning prizes for nosegays of wild and garden flowers. Two years later, there were coconut shies and swingboats at the flower show, as well as dancing and tea. There were 29 prize-winners. A cricket match between Stanton and All Cannings was played on one of Mr Simpkin's fields. Stanton won.

In 1887 Stephen Giddings of Stanton married Rebecca Franklin in the church at All Cannings. They could not afford a 'wagonette' so after the ceremony the bride and groom walked to Stanton to the cottage where they spent their married life and where Stephen died in 1934, aged 81. The newspaper report[118] of his funeral gave details of his life:

> He was born there (in Stanton) and spent the whole of his life in the village; his parents were Mr and Mrs Thomas Giddings. When Stephen was only five years of age his father died, and his early life was one of considerable hardship in those difficult times. At ten years of age he went to work at the Manor Farm. His wages

at first were only 4d per day of ten hours, but circumstances improved and the lad who spent his whole working life on the same farm, ultimately became, for many years, a trusted working foreman. He spent a long period of service with Mr James Tayler, with whom he never lost touch.

Stephen Giddings was a sidesman at the church for many years, then churchwarden. He was a governor of the school for a time and a trustee of the Fowle & Smith charity. For 42 years he was the steward of the Stanton and All Cannings Branch of the Wiltshire Friendly Society. When he retired from the 'Wilts Friendly' aged nearly 80, he was presented with a silver-mounted walking stick and a 'small purse of money' by his fellow parishioners 'as a practical mark of their appreciation'.

When she began to keep house in Stanton, the newly-married Mrs Giddings may have used the shop set up by the Vicar's wife the previous year. Caroline Dixon-Stewart published a letter in the Church Magazine announcing her new venture in August 1886. She was concerned that because many of the labourers' wives had to buy food on credit they were being charged high prices for poor quality goods. The goods in the new shop would be of good quality at much lower prices, but no credit would be allowed. She recognised that it would be difficult initially for some families to escape the burden of debt, but promised that once they had got over the hardship of doing so, they would be much better off. It is thought that a shop existed on the site of *Stoniford House* and *Kelly's Directory* lists two grocers in Stanton in the 1889 edition.

In 1894 the Rev. Dixon-Stewart was made Rector. He continued his practical efforts to improve life for his parishioners by holding a jumble sale in January 1895 to raise money for blankets to lend out to people in the winter. Twenty-eight blankets were purchased and some had been lent out by February.

In the same year he bought and put up in the Rectory grounds the building which became known as the 'Iron Room'. It was soon the centre of social life in Stanton and was put into immediate use for a meeting of the Women's Union and a talk by Rev. H Swanstead on his travels in Palestine. The Church supported the Society for the Propagation of the Gospel and a number of talks were given about foreign countries. A men's club was started in the Iron Room, meeting on several evenings a week, newspapers and a bagatelle board being supplied by the Rector.

Successive vicars and the choir took their music very seriously. In 1889 the magazine notes that at Christmas the anthem 'Behold I bring you good tidings ' was especially well sung, adding:

The singing of the choir of Stanton is very good at all times, and their excellent conduct, attention and regularity, a great encouragement to their vicar, who has diligently trained them for six years.

The congregation apparently agreed because they contributed towards the cost of the annual choir outings. Sometimes these were simply a day out or a cricket match but on two occasions the choir took part in choral festivals in Salisbury and Edington.

The trip to Edington in 1895 started at 9 am when 11 men, 6 boys and the Rector set off in a brake and pair, arriving in good time for dinner in the monastery garden. In the afternoon they amused themselves by 'boating, swinging, etc.' until tea time. Then there was a full rehearsal in the parish church. In the evening, the united choir of 240 voices sang an anthem and choral evensong. After supper, they happily set off home, but 'a choir boy, by accident, rolled down the bank into rather deep water. Our Rector immediately proceeded to his rescue, which he effected successfully, but not without some inconvenience.'

Early in 1898 the church was redecorated and during the summer a mural representing two angels swinging censers was put up on the east wall of the chancel behind the altar. The mural was painted on linen stretched over battens and attached to the wall. The artist was Miss Berry who made no charge for her work, the other expenses being paid by the Rector. In 1900 Miss Berry painted the large mural representing Christ in majesty with saints for the arch between the nave and the chancel, using the same method. The mural was paid for by Mr and Mrs Tayler and Mr Elling (Mrs Tayler's brother) in memory of their mothers. This mural is still in the church and was recently restored, but the angels on the east wall of the chancel were removed some years ago.,

Nothing else is known about Miss Berry and her connections with Stanton. There is a tradition that she was the niece of James Tayler but no evidence of this has been found so far. To be able to execute a work of this size she had definitely received professional training. Because both murals were gifts to the church there are no entries relating to them in the church account book. To add to the mystery, a printed explanation of the Scriptural basis for the mural exists – signed 'H.H.'

In 1888 James Tayler applied to the Charity Commissioners for permission to vary the terms of the Fowle and Smith charity because the trustees thought that there were few opportunities for apprenticing children in a rural community. The Commissioners agreed that whilst apprenticeships were still the primary objective, the funds could also be used for prizes to encourage good school attendance, to make payments to enable children to stay on at school, and to pay for 'outfits' for entering a trade or occupation.[119]

In 1904 the Charity Commissioners held another regular enquiry. The charity was receiving rents from the 36 allotments on its land and had £99 invested. Prizes were being awarded for good attendance at school and sums of 5s were being given each year to girls to buy clothes for starting work as domestic servants. The Rev. Dixon-Stewart reported that 'In a village where the population is mainly engaged in agricultural pursuits there would be difficulty in finding any children who would wish to be apprenticed or could continue at school.'[120]

Thirty years later the vision of Thomas Fowle and Isaac Smith had been so far forgotten that two of the trustees suggested asking the Charity Commissioners whether it was permissible to use the funds for apprenticing boys to an agricultural trade.

By 1903 the motorcar had arrived in Stanton. In December of that year motor vehicle registration became compulsory, and Henry Simpkins was among the first to register his six and a half horsepower Du Pont double phaeton, 'natural wood' in colour, receiving the number plate AM 195. It is estimated that there were about 250 vehicles already on the road in Wiltshire when the Act came into force.[121]

In March 1904 Robbins, Lane and Pinniger acquired a dark green Progress Co. 8 horsepower car, and at about the same time a Singer motorcycle appeared in All Cannings.

In 1906, Henry Simpkins was driving an 8 horsepower Renault with 'red-green' wheels. Five years later, a dashing little 3 horsepower Bédélia, with a 'torpedo shaped body, white with blue lines', could be seen on the drive at Manor Farm House. By 1914, practicality had set in and Henry's vehicle was a 15-20 horsepower Flanders, with a French grey touring body. In the same year, his son Harry bought a 2 horsepower Alldays motorcycle.

The Rev. Dixon-Stewart died in 1905 and the Rev. Edward Montague Parken succeeded him as Rector of Stanton. Faced with the recurring need for money to repair the church, the Rev. Parken realised that to raise the necessary sum he would have to attract donors from outside the village. He decided to hold a Fête and Sale of Work in the Rectory grounds on 19th June 1907. Using his contacts in Wilton, where he had been a curate for some years, he not only borrowed the costumes, script and music of an entertainment called 'A Masque of May Morning' which had already been performed at Wilton House, but persuaded the Countess of Pembroke to come and open the Fête.

In her speech at the Fête the Countess said she had been to Stanton once before to visit the school and the church. She hoped the afternoon would be a 'lovely success'. A bouquet of roses was presented to the Countess by Christine Tayler and Rita Simpkins. The reporter from the *Devizes & Wiltshire Gazette* was clearly puzzled by the presence of the Countess in this 'somewhat isolated village' but

The Old Rectory which was destroyed by fire in 1934

he wrote lyrically about the 'great rounded ramparts of the downs' and the vivid green of the Rectory lawn and shrubbery which made a suitable background for the masque. The girls looked very pretty in their flower costumes, danced gracefully and were quite inaudible, although the reporter put that rather more diplomatically. After the masque the audience went to the 'café chantant' to drink tea to the accompaniment of songs and music.

Mrs Tayler, Mrs Simpkins and Mrs Parken each had a stall, described as an art stall, an advertisement stall and a general stall. There also were buttonholes for sale, a bran tub and a 'four-legged duck'. The reporter thought that the 'district was fairly well represented' and it appears that Rev. Parken was successful in his aim of attracting people from outside Stanton. A profit of £53 12s 8d was made.

Another event had taken place in Stanton that summer. *The Devizes & Wiltshire Gazette* reported on 16th May 1907:

> A highly successful concert was given by Mr & Mrs H Simpkins and their friends in their barn on Monday evening and was well attended. The programme consisted of pianoforte solos by Miss Parry, violin solos by Miss Parken and Mr Bracher, songs by Mrs Parken and Mrs Simpkins, the Rev. E G A Sutton and Messrs W Goddin and Murray Shirriff. The comic element was contributed by Messrs R S Heath and Howard Alexander; the former being such a well-known favourite comment is unnecessary. This was the first public appearance of Mr Alexander on any platform in the character of an entertainer and from the excellent way in which he gave his recitation, we hope to have the pleasure of soon hearing him again. At the conclusion of the concert hearty cheers were given for Mr and Mrs Simpkins, and after singing the National Anthem, the company dispersed.

An item headed 'Alleged theft of firewood' in the *Devizes & Wiltshire Gazette* on 7th November 1907 shows another side of Stanton life.

The question as to how a Stanton woman, named Mary Hill (wife of John Hill) became possessed of five penny worth of firewood occupied the attention of two county magistrates for close upon an hour last Thursday.

The prosecutor was William Rutter, a young man engaged as a groom in the service of Mr James Tayler. From his evidence it appeared that on 29th inst. he was moving his furniture from one house to another, close to that of the prisoner, being assisted by a man called Beavan. The wood, a half-cwt., was put in the woodhouse and was subsequently missed. After searching the premises without being able to find it, witness gave information to P C Holloway, but said nothing to the prisoner about it. When he got back after giving information, the wood was outside his woodhouse in the prisoner's basket.

P C Holloway of All Cannings said on being informed of the loss, he went to Stanton and after making enquiries he went to the prisoner's house. Having cautioned her, he told her he wanted the wood she had taken from Rutter's premises. She replied, 'What wood, I have not taken any wood.' He told her he should search her house and she replied 'You will not search it without a warrant'. He said 'Very well, I will get a warrant and leave someone in charge of the house while I go.' Thereupon the prisoner's husband came in to his dinner, witness explained the facts to him and he gave his consent for the house to be searched. He could find no wood, except some which had evidently been in use for some time to prop up the sofa. However, in the woodhouse the constable found a block of wood which Rutter claimed was his. The rest of Rutter's wood was found outside his house in Mrs Hill's basket. Charged with theft, Mrs Hill's defence was that she had paid the previous tenant (who had moved to London) £1 for 'odds and ends' and she thought the wood had been left for her. The magistrates gave her the benefit of the doubt and dismissed the charge. Mrs Hill worked at home as a laundress; her husband was a gardener.

Forge cottage

The Rev. Parken was rather more strict with the Sunday School children, allowing only those who attended regularly to take part in the treats. However, in 1912 he records a 'Christmas tree' which was popular at a time when few people had one in their own home.

> On Thursday 26th December a Christmas tree was held in the Iron Room at the Rectory for all the children in the village. Each child received a present, a packet of sweets, a cracker, and orange. The school children sang a carol before the distribution of the presents off the tree; the singing was a decided improvement on what we have had on similar occasions. At the conclusion, three hearty cheers were given by the children for those who had so kindly subscribed towards the Christmas tree.

There was again a change of Rector in 1913 when the Rev. Waithman was inducted on Palm Sunday, and briefly resumed the 'Stanton Diary'. He installed a bathroom in the Rectory and when, in the tradition of his predecessors, he began to redecorate, he found he had to strip off as many as 7 layers of wallpaper from some of the walls.

The Rev. Waithman lost no time in organising another garden fête in the grounds of the Rectory:

> Our garden fete and sale of August 26th is over, and we must all feel glad that we can look upon it as a success, owing to the beautiful day and many kind and willing helpers. It was indeed good of the Archdeacon and Mrs Bodington to pay us a visit and show such real interest in our welfare. Mrs Bodington 'opened' the fete at 3 o'clock, but the tennis players had been busy from 11.30. During the afternoon selling was brisk at the stall and many people patronised the concerts and entertainments in the iron room. It was unfortunate that the rain descended a few hours too soon and put a stop to the dancing and incidentally to the illuminations. We have to thank many energetic helpers and those who came from a distance and departed with lighter pockets.
>
> The accounts are as follows:-

RECEIPTS	£	s	d	EXPENDITURE	£	s	d
Stall	10	15	3 ½	Band	1	2	6
Jumble Sale	9	1	9 ½	Refreshments etc.	1	5	10
Refreshments	7	8	3 ½	Illuminations		7	9
Bran pie	1	11	4	Children's prizes		3	0
Gate	6	8	2	Hire (chairs etc.)	1	13	11
Blouse stall	1	6	4	Printing	1	8	6

Tennis tournament	4	0	0	Carting		10	0
Entertainments etc	2	14	1	Balance in hand	36	13	9 ½
	£43	5	3 ½		£43	5	3 ½

A fuller statement of accounts will be found in the church porch.

Part of this money was spent on buying crockery, tablecloths and aprons for the parish and two altar cloths for the church.

Rev. Waithman was a restless man and in the following spring he was organising a parish excursion to the seaside, offering to accept weekly contributions towards the cost so that 'when the time for the excursion comes, our pockets will not seem to suffer so deeply'.

The *Church Magazine* carried the report of the outing:

On Wednesday July 22nd, our much-talked-of parish excursion took place, the population of Stanton having temporarily decreased by 63 people. The choir, most of the school children and many friends and relatives went for the day to Weston-super-Mare, starting by the 7.23 from Woodborough, the children being conveyed in a wagon by Mr Tayler's kindness.

When we arrived at Weston the weather was dull and soon after it began to rain, driving us for shelter under the new pier. Happily it cleared about 1 o'clock, and the rest of the day was beautiful. The children spent their time in digging, paddling, riding donkeys and spending pennies! They had lunch on the sands, and at 5 o'clock fifty of us had tea together in a restaurant. The senior members of the choir enjoyed themselves on the old pier most of the afternoon, trips in a motor boat and on the switchback enlivened the proceedings. We started home at 8.15, being pleased to find that no accidents had happened and that nobody was left behind. We struggled home, tired but triumphant, about midnight.

The day was generally voted to have been a great success and we hope to repeat the experience. We are exceedingly grateful for much kind help that rendered the excursion possible, both for the choir and for the children. Those who went with us and helped indefatigably throughout the day, must have been not a little gratified by the children's keen enjoyment. Perhaps another time many of us will remember that it is easy to be lost in a crowd, that sand thrown in the eyes makes them smart and that sea water is just as wetting as fresh water.

Two weeks later, on 4th August 1914, Britain declared war on Germany.

14
War and the Sale of the Village

AFTER THE DECLARATION of war young men from Stanton joined the tide of volunteers who enlisted from all over the country, motivated by patriotism and a desire for adventure. In October 1914, the parish magazine noted 'we have certainly helped to swell the ranks of Lord Kitchener's army during the last fortnight.' In all, 27 men from Stanton served in the forces during the war.

The Army, faced with the task of accommodating and training this vast influx of recruits, began to build large camps on Salisbury Plain which was its principal training area throughout the war. Constructing the camps and provisioning the troops created civilian jobs which were better paid than agricultural work. There was great activity in Devizes (headquarters of the Wiltshire Regiment) and in the other local towns. Farmers experienced a shortage of manpower, which was to be a growing problem throughout the war.

Horses too were in demand; at the outbreak of war the Army suddenly needed an extra 120,000.[122] Horses were commandeered from farms and private owners, some people giving up their animals voluntarily as a patriotic gesture. As the war continued, more and more animals were needed and the trade in horses was closely regulated.

From the outset, the necessity of increasing food production was recognised. Half the meat and four-fifths of the cereals needed had been imported before the war. Initially, farmers were urged to plough up pasture and plant wheat. As conditions worsened, farming became increasingly regulated. Food prices rose by 133% between 1914 and 1920. Agricultural wages were raised on average to 25 shillings a week by the end of the war but were still well below industrial rates.

For people in Stanton, as everywhere else, there was constant anxiety about relatives and friends serving in the forces. Soon, the Wiltshire Gazette began to publish long casualty lists.

In common with other villages, Stanton was host to a group of Belgian refugees. They were housed 'in a cottage near the smithy which had been furnished for them' and were partially supported by the village during their stay. One of the Belgians was Constant Permeke who later became a leading Expressionist painter.

Throughout the war, the village raised money for charities, mostly by putting on entertainments.[123] The causes supported included the local hospital, the Red Cross, the Serbian Relief Fund, Roehampton Hospital for Limbless Servicemen, and the Wiltshire Prisoners of War Fund. Knitting and sewing groups were organised in the village to make garments for distribution by the Red Cross to hospitals and soldiers at the front and money was raised to buy the necessary materials.

Children in Stanton were involved in the war effort, collecting acorns and chestnuts which were used to produce the acetone needed in the munitions industry. Eggs were collected and sent to hospitals to provide a suitable diet for the wounded men. The dates of school terms were changed to enable children to help on the farms and children played a major part in the fund-raising activities for charities.

As time went on, the Rev. Waithman felt that his parishioners should be better informed about the war. Accordingly, he announced in the parish magazine a series of illustrated lectures on the war, for which he had hired a magic lantern[124] at considerable expense. The entrance charge would be 3d, or 6d for a reserved seat. Unfortunately, in the next issue of the magazine, the Rev. Waithman was grumbling that the lectures had had to be cancelled due to lack of support. Apparently, people had better things to do with their 3d than listen to the parson, whom they could hear for nothing every Sunday. But the Rev. Waithman was no armchair warrior. He had volunteered as a chaplain in the forces and after two years' wait, was eventually called up in 1918, serving at sea and returning in the spring of 1919.

Meanwhile the Rev. Waithman had another cause for annoyance. In the parish magazine for February 1915 he wrote:

> Lord Pembroke's Christmas Gifts. Lord Pembroke sends us £10, half of which is spent on the clothing club in giving 5s. bonuses, and the other half in providing 2cwt. of

coal to as many houses in the village as the money will allow. It is the custom for those who have lived here longest to be provided for first. I strongly deprecate applicants coming to me and saying 'Where is my coal?'

A year later, the Rector was warning people that the price had risen so steeply that Lord Pembroke's money would buy a much smaller quantity of coal for distribution.

In 1915 James Tayler and his wife left Church Farm. The parish magazine states: ' Mr. Tayler has conscientiously and helpfully filled the office of churchwarden for many years, and has set us a good example by his regularity in Church, besides helping the Rector with shrewd advice. Mrs Tayler was a welcome visitor in every cottage, and her quiet and friendly help was greatly appreciated.' Mr Tayler was not only a regular churchgoer himself, but required all his employees to attend also. [125] The Taylers had played a very full part in village life and were generous to the church, donating among other things the pulpit and the font cover. Long after they left the village, the Taylers continued to make gifts to the church at Stanton.

James Tayler's successor at Church Farm was Montague Read. The parish magazine said of him 'Rumour has it that there is not much about farming that he does not know, and he will doubtless prove a worthy successor to Mr. Tayler in other ways as well.' This was true; Monty Read was elected churchwarden and served in that capacity for 50 years. Mr. Read came from Downton near Salisbury, where his family had lived for nearly a hundred years. All his sheep and cattle were transported in one day on the train from Downton to Woodborough station. The animals were driven from there to Stanton and the dairy cattle were milked that night. He was an enterprising and progressive farmer who loved riding and country sports. [126]

Energetic farmers were desperately needed. The poor harvests of 1916 in both Britain and America and the success of the 1916-17 German U–boat campaign in disrupting shipping caused severe shortages, especially of wheat. The scarcity and high cost of food resulted in great hardship in industrial areas. Rationing was introduced to ensure that everyone got at least a basic level of nutrition. Local War Agricultural Committees were set up with powers to enforce the government directives, especially the ploughing up of pasture, and in the last resort to take over inefficient farms.

When conscription was introduced in 1916, some agricultural trades were given exemptions but these were soon withdrawn from single men under 30. To combat the manpower shortage, prisoners of war were available and soldiers were allowed to help with the harvest. A small number of women were trained as milkers at residential schools in the county (the first of these was at Manningford). Once the initial prejudice of some farmers was overcome, the women proved their worth in many tasks. Farmers were more eager to employ boys, campaigning strongly for boys to leave school at 12 to work on the farms.

There were hard frosts during February 1917 and it was officially decided in March to work on Sundays to make up lost time and get the land ploughed and the crops sown. This met with opposition, from A W Perren of Stanton Mill for one. He maintained that 'God promised seed time and harvest and He had not failed yet – provided we as a nation did not walk contrary to Him.'[127]

Monty Read had barely two years to settle in to Church Farm before a truly momentous event occurred in the story of Stanton St Bernard: in 1917 the village was put up for sale by the Pembroke Estate. In addition to its holdings in Stanton, the Estate included in the sale farms at Lea, Cleverton and Overton and part of West Woods, about 3,560 acres in all.

The new Earl had succeeded his father in 1913. Because of increased labour, maintenance and repair costs and a sharp rise in income tax on rents, land was not proving a good investment for the aristocracy and a number of the great estates sold off holdings at this time.[128] In 1915 the Antrobus family sold part of the Amesbury Abbey Estate after the heir to the estate had been killed in action. The sale included Stonehenge which was already a tourist attraction yielding an income of about £360 per annum from visitors.[129]

A prospectus and plans of the properties were prepared and the sale was held over two days. When making up the lots for the sale, land north of the Devizes-Pewsey road had been transferred from Manor Farm to Church Farm, reducing Manor Farm to 503 acres. On Wednesday 27th June 1917 at the 'King's Arms' in Malmesbury, the properties at Lea, Overton and Cleverton were sold. Then the next day, at 3.15 pm on Thursday 28th June, came the turn of 'nearly the whole of the parish of Stanton St Bernard'. The *Wiltshire Gazette* of 5th July carried the following report:

> One of the largest companies which have assembled at a local property sale for many years – probably since the disposal of the Sotheron-Estcourt estate – gathered at the Bear Hotel, Devizes, after market on Thursday, when the Earl of Pembroke's properties lying between Devizes and Marlborough were submitted to auction. The sale was conducted by Mr P M Puckridge (Messrs Ferris & Puckridge of Milton and London) in connection with Messrs Lofts & Warner, surveyors and land agents, of London.

NORTH WILTSHIRE.

In the Malmesbury, Marlborough, and Devizes Districts.

Particulars with Plans and Conditions of Sale

OF THE VERY DESIRABLE

Freehold Agricultural Estates,

Together with Numerous

Accommodation Lands & Small Holdings,

Being more particularly :—

The "Manor" Farm and "Chink" Farm, Lea,

"Street" Farm, Cleverton,

And the Impropriate Tithe Rent Charge in Lea and Cleverton Parish,

Also nearly the whole of

The Parish of Stanton St. Bernard, Pewsey,

With the Manorial Rights and the Advowson of the Living of Stanton St. Bernard,

And the Advowson of North Newnton ;

West Overton Farm, Marlborough,

A portion of the West Woods, and Overton Heath Farm,

The whole extending to

About 3,560 Acres.

FERRIS & PUCKRIDGE

IN CONJUNCTION WITH

LOFTS & WARNER

Have received instructions from Major the Rt. Hon. the Earl of Pembroke and Montgomery to offer the above Valuable Properties for Sale by Auction, as below :—

Lots 1 to 19 at the "King's Arms" Hotel, Malmesbury,

On Wednesday, June 27th, 1917, at 3.30 p.m. precisely ;

Lots 20 to 38 at the "Bear" Hotel, Devizes,

On Thursday, June 28th, at 3.15 p.m. precisely.

Solicitors :
Messrs. NICHOLL, MANISTY & Co.,
1, Howard Street, Strand, W.C. 2.

Auctioneers :
Messrs. FERRIS & PUCKRIDGE,
Milton, Pewsey, Wilts ;
And 79, Queen Street, E.C. 4.

Surveyors and Land Agents :
Messrs. LOFTS & WARNER,
130, Mount Street (corner of Berkeley Square),
London, W. 1.

Cover of the catalogue for the Pembroke Estate sale

The company at the Bear Hotel on Thursday was representative as well as large; it included landowners, agriculturalists with a direct interest in the properties, including some of the tenants, and numerous representatives of the legal profession. In spite of this, however, trade could not be regarded as brisk, though the auctioneer disposed of all the principal lots, and had a prospect of dealing with the smaller parcels privately.

Mr Puckridge made very little ado in opening; after a few terse remarks as to the disposal of the properties on the previous day, and the some score of lots in the catalogue for that day, he proceeded to the direct business of the sale.

The most interesting lot in the sale was what was described as one of the best-noted farms in the Pewsey Vale – Church Farm, Stanton St Bernard, with modern dwelling house, homesteads, cottages and pasture, arable and downland, having a total acreage of just over 1,369 acres. It is let to Mr M J Read, who succeeded Mr James Tayler a few years ago, at an annual rental of £554, which increases to £604 after Michaelmas 1918. Mr Read holds the farm on a lease expiring in 1922, and the whole of the property brings in an annual rental of £707. The tithe rent charge (1917 value) is just over £313. Mr Read put the property in at £8,000, and after a spirited competition it passed into his possession at £11,900. The purchase by Mr Read of the farm of which he is the tenant was greeted with a prolonged round of applause.

The Manor Farm, Stanton St Bernard, consisting of just over 500 acres, with house, buildings and five cottages, let to Mr H J Simpkins and Messrs Robbins, Lane and Pinniger, on yearly tenancies, was started at £5,000 and eventually knocked down to Mr John Nosworthy of Little Cheverell, for £8,100. Practically all this property is in the occupation of Mr Simpkins, at a rental of £250 a year. The tithe rent charge is at present £185 per annum.

The freehold residential property 'The Laurels' (now *Greywethers*) did not sell. Price's Farm (now *Price's Cottage*), at Stanton St Bernard, a small holding of about 6 acres, comprising a dwelling house, building and land, in the occupation of Mr Simpkins, at an apportional rental of £17 a year, with a tithe rent charge of £2, was sold to Mr W B Driver of Cirencester.

Mr M J Read bought six cottages (now *The Row*), together with the homestead known as 'Townsend' (site of *Cherry Tree Lodge*), with an area of about an acre, rented by him and Mr Simpkins at a total of £33 per year, the purchase price being £800. Mr Nosworthy purchased a freehold dwelling house and garden (site of *Glenville*) close to the smithy at Stanton, let to the Rector for £4 a year, for £60. Two other cottages and gardens (now *Fowlers Lane Cottage*), close to Price's Farm, went to the same buyer for £150, and two other cottages (2 *Calf Lane*), bringing in about £5 a year, were bought by Mr Read for £100.

Church Cottage (now *Laburnum Cottage*), Stanton, and two cottages and gardens, paddocks and orchards, let to various tenants at an aggregate apportioned rental of £5.10s a year, did not reach the reserve, and two other cottages (on the site of 7 & 8 *Calf Lane*) let to Mrs Swanborough and Mr A Hams were also unsold.

There was no demand for the manorial rights appertaining to the parish of Stanton St Bernard together with the advowson of the living [right to present a candidate to the ecclesiastical living] and the advowson of the neighbouring parish of North Newnton. There was no bid for the perpetual tithe rent charge of £24 a year payable by the GWR, which the auctioneer said would remain as a good investment for Lord Pembroke.

The total proceeds of the sale were £48,630 (£16,920 at Wednesday's auction, and £31,710 on Thursday).

The auctioneers soon found buyers privately for the unsold properties in Stanton. The prices realised in the sale on Wednesday 27th were: West Overton Farm £8,500, Bell Inn, Overton £700, Park Farm, Overton Heath 116 acres £1,300. 'Sporting woodland' in Fyfield, known as 'Glasses Wood' and 'Puckridge' 275 acres adjacent to West Woods, did not sell and was bought in at £1,250.

The tension felt by bidders, principal tenants and the people of Stanton in the weeks leading up to the sale can be imagined. There must have been general

Mulberry Cottage

relief that Church Farm was sold to a known and respected farmer, but one wonders what Mr. Simpkins and his workers felt, the Simpkins family having lived at Manor Farm since the late 18th century. The sale began a new era for Stanton, which had been administered from Wilton as a single unit for almost a thousand years.

The war continued to drain the country of men and resources. The arrival of a telegram in a yellow envelope was universally dreaded.

Bert Chivers and Dick Norris had been reported missing in 1915 and did not return. Memorial services were held for Archibald Pearce and Frederick Doggett. Albert Bristow was reported killed.[130]

People's daily lives were affected in many mundane ways. British Summer Time had been introduced, against opposition from many of the farming community. All possible space in gardens was being used to grow vegetables. The parish magazine notes the lack of flowers for decorating the church, and that 'the claims of potatoes now come before the claims of choir practice'. Due to a deficit in church funds, caused by the 'expense of darkening the church', the organist repaid part of her annual fee.

The hated 'grey loaf' had been introduced. It was made using the minimum of wheat flour with the addition of whatever other grains were available. Bread could not be sold in Wiltshire until it was at least 24 hours old, presumably so that it could be sliced more thinly. In July, Stanton people were warned of the scarcity of coal in the coming winter and were advised to buy supplies early if possible. Lord Pembroke would no longer be sending his Christmas gift of £10 for coal and the clothing club.

Finally, 11th November 1918, the Armistice was declared. Demobilisation was slow, but eventually the men began to come home to take up their lives again as best they could, changed by their experiences. This was a difficult time for the families of those who had died as they felt their loss acutely in the midst of the general relief and rejoicing. The Doggett family at the Barge Inn was particularly hard-hit. Mrs Doggett lost two sons in the war and her husband died soon afterwards in 1920. Three prisoners of war returned in February 1919; Arthur Tayler, Ernest Jackman and Jack Norris who had been a prisoner for 4 years, part of that time in Russia where he had lost a hand. Jack Norris awed local children with his ability to catch a rat with his prosthetic hook.[131]

The Rev. Waithman came back, still grumbling, this time about the war memorial that Mr and Mrs Simpkins had erected in the church, which he said was 'put up against my wishes while I was serving'.[132] The Simpkins said they wanted to do this before they left Manor Farm, as they had known the men who had served since they were boys. The Simpkins' war memorial is on the wall opposite the door, and contains two names which do not appear on the memorial put up by the village.[133]

On 19th July 1919 there were peace celebrations. The children marched through the village waving flags and were treated to a tea. Later, Mr Read lit a bonfire on the hill. 'Partly owing to the weather and partly owing to the fact that town attractions proved too strong, the proceedings in the evening for adults were limited to a very small number. However, we managed to enjoy ourselves, even on the top of the downs at midnight on a decidedly bleak summer's evening.'[134]

The attraction in Devizes which lured people away was a procession of floats organised by the staff of Wadworths, W E Chivers and E & W Anstie which toured the town. It started at 9 pm and was headed by a woman dressed in white representing 'Peace'. The floats illustrated various aspects of the war, including the allied countries. A dance which had been planned in the open air was hastily transferred to the Corn Exchange because of the rain, the music being provided by the band of the 1st Wiltshire Regiment.

It was decided that, besides putting up a village war memorial, 'framed momentoes' would be given to the ex-soldiers and bereaved families. At least two of these survive: those presented to T J Price and A Clifford. They were patriotic watercolours showing regimental badges and military vignettes, painted by the Misses Garrett.

An account of the dedication of the war memorial tablet is given in the parish magazine in 1920. 'It must be seldom that the Church has been better filled than it was on the evening of February 29th. Most of the Stanton men who served were present to pay respect to the memory of the honoured dead. The service was all that it should have been – quiet, reverent and well rendered by the choir. The Rural Dean preached a most helpful and sympathetic sermon. The tablet to the fallen, which is placed on the wall near the pulpit and is of brass on grey marble, bears the following inscription: 'To the glorious memory of the men from this parish who fell in the Great War 1914-1918. Albert Bristow, Albert Chivers, Herbert Crook, Frederick Doggett, Tom Doggett, Richard Norris, Archibald Pearce, Frederick Snook.'

15
Twenty Years of Peace

L IFE GRADUALLY returned to normal. The wet summer of 1920 affected the school holidays as the children were needed to help with haymaking. 'The rain has kept the hay about a long time and not improved its quality. It has also rather upset our arrangements for the summer holidays. However, we are now trying the experiment of having holidays if fine; if wet the bell rings and school is as usual'.[135]

There were weddings, including those in 1919 of Monty Read to Miss Sawtell, the daughter of a 'feather purifier' of Melksham, and of Ivo Perry to Fanny Giddings. About 250 people attended a big concert was held in the barn at Manor Farm. In March 1920, the ailing church organ 'seized this opportunity to give out'. 'The choir (to say nothing of the organist) has been bravely struggling under adversity of late'. It was decided to have the organ repaired and raise the money (£20) afterwards by holding a fete.[136]

There were still shortages but Stanton people were determined to enjoy life. A cricket club was started in 1921. Mr Lawrence (who had succeeded Mr Simpkins at Manor Farm) lent his 'large field'. The club had 35 members, the subscription being 4s for the men and 1/6d for the boys. The parish magazine notes: 'more keenness than science prevails, but if the former continues, the latter ought soon to develop'. The new football club did better. By December 1922 it had played seven matches – 1 lost, 1 drawn and 5 won. The Captain was Mr E Pearce and the Secretary Mr F Nash.

The military authorities had closed many of the camps on Salisbury Plain and were selling off buildings and equipment. Monty Read bought a large hut from Ludgershall and on 14th November 1921 'an excellent concert was given in Mr Read's army hut by the 'Pewsey Revellers' – Mr Tom Billington and his friends. The audience, which must have numbered over 200, was very appreciative. Proceeds to the upkeep of the school – £5.15.10d.'

The following March a lanternslide lecture was given in the Iron Room for the Sunday School children, but the atmosphere was so damp that the lens kept fogging up. 'Despite these drawbacks, the show was appreciated.' There was dancing in the Iron Room on Thursday evenings. In November, the Harvest Festival was apparently a success – 'good congregation on the Sunday, and I think we have never sent more to the hospital'.[137]

At Easter in 1923 the church was decorated with an 'abundance of spring flowers' and there were almost 50 communicants. 'The choir had been hard at work for some time on the Easter music, especially a new anthem of Stainer's. This was the most ambitious thing we have attempted, at any rate in the present Rector's time; and the rendering of it reflected the greatest possible credit on the choir and organist alike. Altogether, with beautiful weather and cheerful services, a very happy Easter.'[138]

In August there were very few entries from Stanton in the All Cannings and Stanton flower show, but 'we have to record one well-deserved first prize for Stanton, Mr and Mrs Ivo Perry's baby being awarded the prize for being the finest specimen of humanity of tender years'.[139]

Miss Rogers, the head teacher at the school (and also church organist) left the village in 1924. Her house was needed for a farm worker and efforts to obtain money from the Diocese to build a new house for her had failed, although Monty Read had offered to provide the land. Her leaving present from the village was a 'serviceable-looking bicycle'. Soon afterwards, the County Council began a programme of house building in the villages, including eight houses in Stanton. These are 7 and 8 Church Road and 1 to 6 Coate Road. The cost was given as £439 for the 'non-parlour' type, and £510 for the 'parlour' type.[140]

Farming was still a mix of arable, dairy and the sheep which were folded to manure the land. Most of the feed for cattle was grown on the farms. Milking was done by hand and the full churns were taken in the evening by horse and cart to Woodborough station. It was estimated that about 10 cows could be milked in an hour and a gang of milkers came in to do the job.[141] Feed for the sheep was grown, the animals being put into the fields to graze the crop. Sonny Perry started work with the shepherd at Church Farm in 1938 when he left school. One of his first tasks was to carry the hurdles and help to construct the folds which had to be moved daily.

A large workforce was needed. For example, using the traction engine, about eleven men were needed to thresh a rick of wheat, the aim being to complete the job in a day. A good rick would yield about 80 sacks of wheat and straw in bales, which then would be hauled away by horse and cart. Many of the workers were 'day men', who were set on to do tasks as required: threshing, dung spreading, harvesting and fencing. Then there were the specialists: shepherds, milkers and dairymen, carters, the traction engine driver. [142]

Church Farm Dairy, now Pewsey Vale Riding School

A pair of steam ploughing engines had been in use at Church Farm for some years before the war. There was also a steam traction engine which was used for baling, threshing and other stationary work. But when these machines were working, horses were still needed to haul the fuel and water needed to keep them going. Jim Read, Monty Read's son, remembered 21 working heavy horses at Church Farm, in addition to a number of lighter horses. The forge was a busy place, employing a farrier to shoe the horses, and a blacksmith to make and repair tools and machinery. One of the blacksmith's jobs was to fit the iron tyres on to the wooden wheels and one of the circles on which the wheel was laid for this process can still be seen in the children's playground.

Monty Read, for one, was keen to adopt modern methods and by 1930 had a number of tractors. He installed a generator at Church Farm to supply the farm with electricity. In about 1928, he built a narrow gauge (2 ft) railway which ran from the Devizes-Pewsey road (opposite the bus stop at the eastern exit from Stanton) up the track to the milking parlour at 'Tin Town' below Milk Hill. The locomotive was a petrol-driven Lister, as used on railway platforms, but adapted for rail work.[143] The railway was used to take feed up and bring down the full milk churns which were then loaded on to a lorry and taken to Woodborough station. The railway track was lifted in about 1954.

Although most people got around by bicycle, motor transport was changing rural life. A bus service to Devizes replaced the carrier's horse and cart. The Devizes-Pewsey road was metalled and in 1924 a signpost to Stanton was erected, an indication of people's growing mobility. Among others, the Rev Waithman acquired a car. He 'enlarged the garage at a cost of £15' in 1923 and the following year contributed to the cost of having the road surfaced 'from Coate Lane to our gates'. New possibilities for leisure were opened up by the coach outings and 'mystery tours' run by the Popes of Alton Barnes. In 1932 Tan Hill Fair was moved to a site near Silbury Hill on the London to Bath road, because lorries could not negotiate the tracks up Tan Hill.

On 25th June 1925 the Rev. Waithman took his last Sunday service in Stanton and left to become Rector of Winterslow. He had been an energetic presence in Stanton and his trenchant comments lent colour to the parish magazine. He was succeeded by the Rev. Sydney Lambert.

During the summer the 'Parish Room', usually called the 'Iron Room', was moved by volunteers from the garden of the Rectory and was enlarged and re-erected on the site now occupied by 'Langdale'.[144] The men's club used the Iron Room on three evenings a week for billiards and skittles. For the women, there was the Women's Institute and Mothers' Union, with meetings alternating between Stanton and Alton Barnes.

At the Easter Vestry meeting in 1926 'the subject of the cobbles in the church path was again raised by Miss Stirling and others'. After much discussion it was decided to ask Mr Gimson to make enquiries about the possibility of 'smoothing over the cobbles with cement or asphalt' for a cost of £10 or less. Apparently Mr Gimson's enquiries were unsuccessful, because the problem is still with us.

In 1928 electric lighting was installed in the church. This was powered by the Church Farm generator which charged a bank of batteries ranged along the wall inside the church.[145] The cost (£53 11s 3d) was largely met by the Rev. and Mrs Lambert, with £11 4s 6d being collected from the parish and Mr Read contributing £3 4s 9d plus £2 2s 0d for the meter. The graceful but messy oil lamps were removed; some were used in the Iron Room and the rest were stored in the Rectory. On 13th January 1929 the first service lit by electric light was conducted in Stanton church. The following year, the running cost of the electric light was found to be £1 5s 0d over 12 months, against £1 7s 0d for oil and candles for the previous year. In 1932 Mr Read pointed out at the Vestry Meeting that it was advisable to run the generator sometimes on Sundays and it was agreed to pay an honorarium of 10 shillings to Mr Frank Nash 'for performing this service'.

Monty Read's father-in-law, Henry Sawtell, was very successful with hare coursing. He won a number of trophies, including the Waterloo Cup twice and also raced his dogs at White City in London. He trained his greyhounds on the 'dog run' below Milk Hill, between the square areas of trees which can still be seen there. The hares were penned into the wooded areas using netting and then released when the dogs were ready.

Winter was the season for shooting partridges, about 25 brace being shot on a good day. Monty Read invited other local farmers who assembled at the Army Hut for a glass of sherry. Later the guns had a hot lunch in the hut, with the beaters getting corned beef sandwiches, pickled onions and beer. In the evening the farmers returned to Church Farm with their wives for supper (often a couple of geese) and a game of cards. Each farm would hold a shoot about twice in a season.[146] Beating on the shoots and hare coursing provided extra work for the farm workers.

The hunting season started in November. Monty Read, a keen huntsman, kept his own hunters but many farmers used their working horses, some taking the milk to the station in the morning and hunting on the same horse in the afternoon.

Rabbits were abundant on top of Milk Hill and near Wansdyke. Three or four rabbit catchers were employed during the winter months to trap the rabbits which were crated up and sent by train to Smithfield Market. Between 10 and 20 thousand rabbits would be caught during the season.[147]

Winters were more severe at this time and the canal regularly froze over. The children enjoyed sliding and playing hockey on the frozen canal which was of course still normally used for commercial traffic. For the more fortunate children, the blacksmith made skates.

Another diversion had made its appearance in Stanton, putting it in direct touch with the wider world. On his retirement in 1932, the Rev. Lambert was presented with a 'handsome wireless set'. Only Church Farm had an electricity supply: the wireless sets were powered by 'accumulators', large glass jars which were rechargeable batteries and which had to be taken to Church Farm to be charged up.

The Rev. Lambert's retirement marked a major change: the parish of Stanton was united with Alton Barnes. As the new Rector, Rev. Nathaniel Jenkins, lived at Alton, Stanton Rectory was put up for sale. It was still empty and on the market in January 1934 when it was gutted by fire. Mr D Pearce, who acted as caretaker, had lit a slow combustion stove in order to air the house and it was thought that the stove pipe overheated, setting fire to the first floor which then ignited the stairway. The fire was not noticed until the following morning. The fire brigade was called by telephone. Water was brought from the canal but by this time the heat was so intense that the firemen could not approach the building. 'A rain of tiles and slates from the roof which had become red hot slid to the ground in large quantities.'

Only a part of the kitchen wing could be saved. According to the *Wiltshire Gazette*, a passer-by had seen a light in one of the bedrooms of the empty house at 11 pm 'but was under the impression that this was due to someone examining the house'.[148] This was the second serious fire in Stanton since the war: Mr Lawrence's barns on the north side of Manor Farm House had been burned down in December 1923.

The Rectory fire was the first time a telephone had been used in Stanton to summon the fire brigade. A few telephones had been installed by 1931 but for most people the only telephone available was the public one in Miss Hillier's post office and grocery shop. When the Post Mistress received a call for someone in the village, she would send one of the children with a message for the person concerned. The bus service had improved access to Devizes for shopping and this, together with more adequate wage rates, meant that the old clothing club was no longer needed. Bread was delivered daily from Honey Street. People of course mostly relied on their gardens for vegetables.

From 1936, the land behind Canal Cottages and Hillview, bounded by the canal, the Alton Barnes road and the Devizes road, was used by the RAF Central Flying School, based at Upavon, as a practice landing ground. The biplanes, first Avro 504Ns and later Avro Tutors, enlivened the Stanton scene as the trainee instructors practised forced landings and circuits. The grass field, known as the Alton Barnes landing ground, was equipped only with a windsock, but was relatively easy to locate using the white horse and the canal as reference points.[149]

The Coronation of King George VI in l937 was celebrated in traditional style. There were sports for children and adults followed by tea in Mr Read's army hut when every child was given a commemorative mug. During the sit-down dinner in the hut in the evening everyone listened to the broadcast of the King's speech and then had a party.[150]

The international situation became more and more threatening. After the Munich crisis in 1938 the authorities, using their experience of only 20 years before, prepared the country for war. Once again Salisbury Plain and the garrison town of Devizes buzzed with military activity. Early in 1939 camps were built

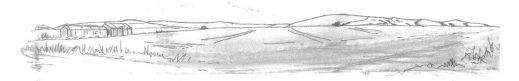

Monty Read's hut is the building nearest the Devizes road

along London Road to house the men conscripted into the militia for six months' training. This time the whole population would be mobilised from the outset. People were urged to join the forces or the emergency services; men under 35 were conscripted from 1939 and women from 1941.

The new threats were aerial bombardment and gas attacks. Everyone was issued with a gas mask to carry at all times; young children were given a gas mask with coloured ears and a tongue which was supposed to resemble Mickey Mouse. The gas masks had been developed at Porton Down. Air raid shelters were built in towns and arrangements made to evacuate children from the towns to rural areas. A mock air-raid exercise was held in Avebury on 8th July 1939 complete with blackout, 'bombs' which failed to explode due to the damp weather and mock casualties taken to the first aid depot.[151]

At 11.15 am on 3rd September 1939 people all over Britain heard on their wireless sets the bleak voice of Neville Chamberlain announcing that the country was again at war with Germany.

16
The Second World War

OR FOUR DAYS from 1st September two trains a day carrying evacuees from London arrived in Devizes, a total of 800 children in groups of 50 with one teacher to each group. The children carried a few belongings and a gas mask. They were given rations for 24 hours, then taken to the Corn Exchange to be allocated to foster parents in Devizes and the villages. Stanton received 15 children on the second day and 14 on the fourth day.

Mothers with very young children also came to Wiltshire from London. One mother and her children was housed in 2 Calf Lane with very little furniture – some boxes and an old Victorian sofa.[152] Other evacuees were accommodated in the thatched cottage formerly on the site of 1 Reads Close. Three boys lodged for a while with Mrs Shaw and her daughter Lil Hams in Corner Cottage (then two houses).[153] Foster parents could claim a weekly allowance of between 10s.6d. and 15s. depending on the age of the child. When the expected heavy bombing did not immediately occur, some evacuees decided to return home, but after bad raids on London and on the ports in 1940, another wave of evacuees arrived in Devizes.[154] However some of the evacuees stayed in Stanton for a considerable time and attended the village school.

Blackout regulations were enforced from the declaration of war. Tommy Smith the blacksmith was the air-raid warden in Stanton. Car headlights and bicycle lamps were masked so that only a strip of light emerged and every house had to put up black curtains at the windows. With no public electricity supply in Stanton, these restrictions were not as onerous as in town but the proximity of the Alton

Barnes landing ground no doubt ensured that the blackout was strictly observed. With the urgent need to train more pilots and instructors the airfield was increasingly busy. The White Horse, a very obvious landmark, was turfed over.

The government took immediate control of the food supply, imposing rationing and setting up local War Agricultural Committees with wide powers, as in the last war. There was again a manpower shortage on the farms although agriculture was a reserved occupation. There had been some mechanisation since the last war but horses still predominated. Monty Read had purchased a second-hand 'International' combine harvester in 1939, one of the first in the area to do so[155]. It was assembled by a man called Johnny Johnson, who arrived in his own light aircraft which landed near the canal. Once the war started petrol was rationed; farmers and other essential users had an allowance of 'red' petrol. Anyone caught using red petrol for private motoring was liable to a prison term.

By November 1939, at least five Stanton men[156] were on active service or training and it is thought that about ten served in the forces during the war.[157] Women were not conscripted until 1942 but from the start of the war many women joined the forces or were directed into factory work. There were Stanton women in the ATS (Auxiliary Territorial Service), the Land Army and in local factories, including the flax factory on London Road, Devizes which produced webbing. [158]

Women were busy on the 'home front' also. In the autumn of 1939 the Stanton and Alton WI held a whist drive which raised £3.0s.4d. for materials for the Red Cross Working Party and by April 1940 over 200 'comforts for the troops' had been made by members: 121 pairs of mittens, 7 pairs of operation stockings, 17 pairs of gum boot stockings, 35 scarves, 4 pairs of bedsocks, 2 pullovers and 2 body belts.

The local WI joined the national scheme for making jam from surplus fruit, for which an extra sugar ration was allowed, and produced 500 lbs of jam in 1940 and 200 lbs in 1941, much of it gooseberry. Naturally there was great emphasis at WI meetings on making the best use of available food. One talk mentioned in the parish magazine was on 'Vegetables in wartime' held at Laburnum Cottage on 1st October 1941. Stanton people undoubtedly fared better than townspeople, as they were accustomed to producing their own vegetables and eggs but they experienced the same shortages of imported goods. Everyone was urged to 'Dig for Victory' and grow as much food as possible in their gardens and allotments.

On 14th May 1940 Anthony Eden, acceding to the demand from men not eligible to serve in the forces but keen to 'do their bit', announced the formation of the 'Local Defence Volunteers'. Within 24 hours, around 250,000 men had volunteered and by the end of June the number had risen to nearly one and a half million, of whom about half had served in the First World War. The government was unprepared for this huge response and had no equipment for the new LDV, whose name was quickly changed to 'The Home Guard' after jokes that the initials stood for 'Last Desperate Venture' or 'Look, Duck and Vanish'.[159]

Although Stanton was in the Devizes Rural District Council area, it was included in the 10th Battalion of the Wiltshire Home Guard whose boundaries were those of the Pewsey RDC. This was to avoid having two battalions jointly responsible for the defence of the Alton Barnes landing ground. Stanton volunteers joined the company which also covered Alton Barnes, Oare and Wilcot. The Rev. Nathaniel Jenkins initially led the platoon of his parishes of Stanton and Alton Barnes, but 'with the coming of Sunday parades and being somewhat elderly he regretfully handed over to a younger man'. Though there was training and exercises were held (timed to fit in with milking), for over a year few weapons were available. The national average was one rifle for every six men. Molotov cocktails were the most accessible weapon. Eventually, the government issued pikes which the Commanding Officer of the 10th Battalion refused to accept, saying 'if it comes to it they would do far better with hay forks'.[160]

After the period of the 'phoney war' came the defeats in Norway and in France. Men of the local regiments were evacuated from Dunkirk in May 1940. Their return to Devizes, exhausted, dishevelled and without weapons, brought home vividly to everyone the real possibility of a German invasion. On 20th July 1940 Hitler issued his Directive, 'Preparations for the invasion of Britain', known as Operation Sealion.

General Ironside, commander-in-chief of home forces, fortified the Kennet and Avon Canal as a second line of defence in the event of a German invasion force making a successful landing on the south coast. The aim was to delay the German advance for long enough to give British troops time to converge on the area under attack. The pillboxes, constructed by local builders, can still be seen in the fields beside the canal and along the Devizes to Pewsey road. Anti-tank blocks, made from sewer pipes filled with concrete, were placed on the bridges over the canal. (The one on Stanton Bridge is still there in the hedge, but covered now with ivy.) Signposts were

Pillbox

removed. Instructions were given
to the population about what to do
if the Germans invaded. The signal
that an invasion had occurred
would be the ringing of church
bells.

Gun emplacement

There was also the fear that the Germans would mount an air-borne invasion. If this happened it would be vital to deny them the use of the airfields. Concrete gun emplacements were built beside the Alton Barnes landing ground. After a German bomber dropped three bombs on the field between Stanton House and the canal opposite the landing ground during the night of 14th September the defences were reinforced by the construction of more gun emplacements.

While all this defensive building work was proceeding on the ground in the fine summer weather of 1940, the Battle of Britain was being fought in the skies over southern England. Nothing could have demonstrated more clearly that the war could only be won with air superiority.

Training of aircrew had high priority and more qualified instructors were needed. The use of the Alton Barnes landing ground increased still further. Unfortunately there was no flying control, only a 'loose priority system' for take-offs and landings which resulted in accidents. On 18th June 1941 there was a collision in which both crews were killed. On 4th September 1941 another accident cost the lives of two airmen.[161]

At the end of 1941, the Alton Barnes landing ground was placed under the control of the new No.29 Elementary Flying Training School (EFTS) which had been set up at Clyffe Pypard in September. Alton Barnes was upgraded to a Relief Landing Ground. Air-raid shelters and ten blister hangars were constructed, as well as buildings for training purposes sited along the Honey Street-Alton Barnes road. No.29 EFTS, which was operated by a civilian flying school, taught basic flying skills plus navigation, radio communication and photography. The course initially lasted six months but was reduced to four months as the demand for pilots increased. The first course took 71 students, flying Tiger Moths and Magisters.

In June 1942 No.29 EFTS was enlarged from four training flights to six, Alton Barnes becoming the base for the two extra flights. Pre-glider courses were also provided for the Army. To cope with the resulting congestion an airfield controller was appointed to control take-offs and landings, signalling to the aircraft with an Aldis lamp. On 16th April 1942 the rendezvous lights, which had been placed on Milk Hill for night flying exercises, were mistaken for a night bombing range by an aircraft from an Operational Training Unit and a stick of small bombs was dropped on the hill.

The soft sticky ground on the landing field had always been a problem. After heavy rain in the winter of 1943/4, a perimeter track of metal 'Somerfield' tracking was laid. By this time, the field behind Stanton House on the opposite side of the road leading to Mill Farm was also being used as a dispersal area.[162]

Meanwhile, Stanton people continued with their busy lives, accustomed to the sound of aircraft overhead. It was a time when people's lives were closely regulated on the one hand, but on the other there were unprecedented chances to break normal rules and conventions. At least one Stanton resident was taken up on an unauthorised flight from the airfield and there is the tale of a trainee pilot who flew a Tiger Moth through one of the hangars.

Tragedy was never far away. In 1942 two Stanton men died in Burma: Leslie Waters, 2nd Royal Tank Regiment RAC, on 2nd March and Frederick Price, 1st Battalion Gloucestershire Regiment, on 2nd May. As in the previous war, farmers were required to cultivate every possible piece of land. The Agricultural Committee sent out heavy-duty tractors from Devizes to clear the scrub and plough up the grassland on the tops of the hills. Dairy farming was of special importance. Farming

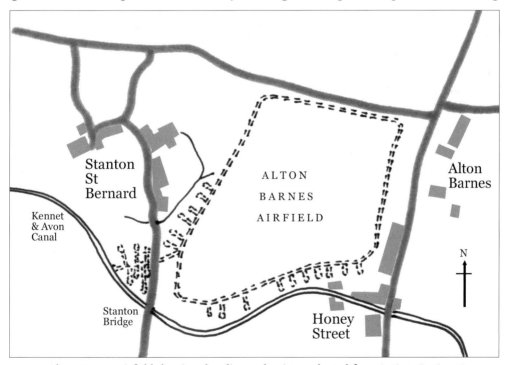

Alton Barnes airfield showing the dispersal points (adapted from Action Stations*)*

was still labour-intensive by modern standards: in 1942 twenty-nine people were employed at Stanton Dairy.[163] Milking was still done by hand. Sonny Perry, who was a milker, remembers carrying the milk in two pails suspended from a yoke slung across his shoulders. Sonny served in the Home Guard but missed parades and exercises if they coincided with milking times.

Because of the labour shortage, local women were employed on the farms in Stanton. The Women's Land Army played an important role nationally and some local girls joined. A Land Girl who came to Stanton was Barbara Jameson, a vicar's daughter, who worked at Church Farm and married Monty Read's son Jim in 1947.

Help was also provided by seven Italian prisoners of war, then lodged in the thatched cottage on the site of 1 Reads Close. They became part of village life, especially when some of their wives joined them. In 1943, after their country joined the Allies, the Italians became 'co-belligerents' and continued to help the British war effort. Some of the Italians made their homes in Wiltshire when the war ended. 'Sarge' Abbandonato eventually bought *The Mansion*. One German prisoner of war came to Stanton from the large POW camp on the London Road in Devizes. Known as 'Happy', he worked at Manor Farm and lived in a double-decker bus in the yard there.[164] He stayed in Wiltshire after the war and married a local girl.

Early in 1943, a new Rector was installed, Rev. J M L F McAnally. He stated his intention to set up an electoral roll of church members, and to 'revive' the choir in Stanton. By the summer, there were 86 people on the roll in Alton and 96 in Stanton and church councils had been elected in both villages. A Free Will Offering Scheme was started, requiring regular donations from people on the roll, but after that there were no further entries in the parish magazine for Stanton for the next three years.[165]

By this time the Home Guard was properly equipped and in April 1943 was put on special alert against the threat of enemy parachutists, which was a recurring fear throughout the war. If a Home Guard witnessed the descent of four (later increased to 25) enemy parachutists, he was to toll the church bell, or to do so on the orders of a Home Guard officer or Police Constable. In 1944, the Home Guard was put in charge of guarding the railway stations.[166]

In the build up to the Allied invasion, the arrival of the glamorous American troops, with their gifts of chewing gum and nylon stockings, caused the same stir in Stanton as it did everywhere else. They were stationed in Devizes and at RAF Upavon. Throughout the war, social activities had been organised in Devizes to entertain the British and overseas soldiers based in the town. Stanton girls, wearing their evening dresses, would cycle to Devizes or to Upavon for the dances held there. There was at least one GI bride from Stanton.[167]

In early 1944, convoys were moving south and intense preparations for the Allied invasion were being made, but no one knew exactly when it would take place. The Home Guard was ordered to stand to with arms and ammunition. On 6th June 1944 the announcement was made on the wireless that 'allied troops have landed on the coast of France'. A Stanton man was among them: T J Price who survived in spite of losing his kit whilst under attack as he came ashore. After serving in the First World War, Thomas Price had signed on as a regular soldier and was posted to India between the wars.

Once the Allied forces were established in Europe, the Home Guard was no longer needed and was stood down. The final parade of the 10th Battalion was held in the Pewsey cinema in November 1944.[168]

The announcement of 'Victory in Europe' was made on 8th May 1945, but it was not until three months later that the war in the Far East ended and V-J Day was marked on 15th August. A thanksgiving service for victory was held in the church on 8th May, followed by a 'National Service' for the Home Guard on 13th May, which must have been very well attended because the collection was the unusually large sum of £2.12.0d.[169] Naturally, Stanton marked V-E Day with a big party in the black hut: a trailer was sent round the village beforehand to collect enough chairs to seat everyone. Some returning servicemen received a very warm welcome: Frank Beaven came home wearing a 'big hat with the side turned up'. His family had put up plenty of flags – even the apple tree was decorated – cakes had been made and there was a party.

The Alton Barnes Landing Ground had fulfilled its purpose. On 7th July 1945 its aircraft were flown back to Clyffe Pypard. The field was put under 'care and maintenance' but was used on a few occasions to practice forced landings until it was returned to farmland in 1947. Now only pillboxes and the concrete bases of gun emplacements are visible in the field beside the canal. One building remains beside the Alton Barnes-Honey Street road and a memorial has been put up on the nearby air raid shelter to commemorate the RAF presence during the war and those who died in training accidents.

The names of the two Stanton men who died in Burma, Frederick Price (brother of T J Price) and Leslie Waters, were added to the War Memorial in the church.

17

Great Changes

E VERYWHERE the servicemen came home in their new 'demob' suits and
tried to adapt to the routine of their former lives, not without difficulty for
those who had been away for four or five years. The many young women
who had served in the forces or who had done 'men's work' on the farms and in
the factories found their job opportunities once again restricted to traditional
female roles. The war had changed people's attitudes and the unexpected Labour
victory in the 1945 election showed a national determination to improve living
conditions.

People were exhausted by five years of war; the shortages and food rationing
continued. The winter of 1946-7 was especially cold and harsh: fuel, household
goods and clothes were in very short supply. Women leaving the Land Army were
careful to keep the thick greatcoats which had been issued to them. Blackout
curtains were cut up to make skirts, enlivened by rows of coloured braid and
parachute silk was eagerly purchased, when obtainable, to make underwear and
dresses for the many post-war weddings.

Stanton was about to experience perhaps the greatest period of change in its
long history. This meant first of all the provision of basic amenities. In 1943 mains
electricity had been provided to Church Farm and to the new pair of houses, 9
and 10 Church Road, which were built in that year. In 1948 an overhead power
supply was at last brought to the whole village, but each house was given only a
lighting circuit to light the rooms, not the hall or landing, and with two sockets,
one upstairs and one downstairs, which people mostly used for their radios. Stanton

people still had to wait for labour-saving items such as electric fires, irons and kettles, which (anyway) were expensive and in short supply. But it was a great improvement and the children were thrilled, rushing outside at dusk to look at the lighted windows.

The new National Health Service established in 1946 benefited everyone. Now people could consult a doctor and get the treatment they needed without worrying about having enough money to pay the bill.

Stanton was still mostly dependent on well water. Some houses had hand pumps but for many people filling buckets was a daily chore. Joyce Hale remembers that after school each day her task was to fill two buckets from the well for a neighbour, who gave her two tiny cough sweets in return. When the elderly couple living in Rose Cottage could not get to their well because of thick snow, they filled their buckets with the snow and let it melt. In the larger houses water was pumped up from the wells into water tanks. Church Farm had its own water supply by 1917 and bathrooms had been installed there and at Manor Farm in the early 1900s. When the Milk Marketing Board was set up in the 1930s the dairy farmers needed large quantities of pure water to meet its standards and bulk supplies of water were brought in for them from Devizes. In 1956 water was piped to the village from a borehole at Bourton near Bishops Cannings. Initially the water supply to some of the houses was from standpipes, one shared between three houses.

In 1958 a sewage treatment plant was built on the parish boundary north of the canal, near Englands Bridge. Monty Read had all his estate houses connected to the sewer; other householders were asked to pay £50 for the connection but not everyone took up the option at the time. Of those who did, no one regretted the replacement of the old earth closets with the luxurious new flushing lavatories. When the electricity supply was up-graded later, electric cookers, washing machines and modern bathrooms could be installed. Gone were the weekly baths taken in the big galvanised iron tub in front of the living room fire.

Gone too was the great upheaval of washing day, when on Sunday evenings the built-in copper in the kitchen or outhouse was filled with water, the sheets and towels were put in to soak and the fire was lit under the copper. By morning the water was boiling. The washing was fished out using wooden tongs, rinsed in the sink and wrung out with the big mangle which was turned by hand, often by a conscripted child. More washing was put in and there was steam everywhere. Finally, advantage was taken of the hot water to scrub the kitchen table and wash the steps.

Coal was delivered by Robbins, Lane and Pinniger but it continued to be expensive and wood was, as ever, in short supply. People still went 'wooding' in the southern part of the village. Gardens and allotments provided most of the vegetables. Mr King was the milkman; customers had to have their jugs ready and the milk would be poured in using quart, pint or half-pint measures dipped in to the churn. There were regular deliveries to the village: Vigors with meat, Mr Long from Patney with fish, Lewis with groceries every Friday, the 'Tizer man' with soft drinks, Slades of Devizes with hardware and paraffin. Strongs and the Co-op between them delivered bread every day. Slopers came with clothes from Devizes and Mr Bartlett from Pewsey brought underwear and clothing. Dodges brought shoes from their shop in the Brittox.

There was of course the village shop and post office which was run by Miss Bishop until 1968, when Mr and Mrs Hampshire took over the business. Mrs Perry made wedding and bridesmaids dresses for village weddings. In later years, Percy Goss sold vegetables from his garden where *Glenville* now stands. Arthur Bailey sold soft drinks from his house in The Row.

There was a bus service to Devizes at 10 a.m. on Tuesdays and Thursdays, returning at 2 p.m. on Tuesday and 3.30 p.m. on Thursday, market day. Buses ran all day on Saturdays for shopping and for the cinema, waiting until the film finished to take the passengers home. With few cars on the road bicycles were widely used to get to work and for shopping. Mrs Perry used to go shopping to Devizes on her bicycle, returning with a full shopping bag on each handlebar. People cycling to Devizes to see a film could leave their bicycles in the yard of the *Black Swan* or at *The Three Crowns* if they were going to the Regal Cinema on the site of *Chantry Court*.

The men's club continued to meet in the Iron Room in the evenings for talk and billiards, provided the stove had been lit beforehand. There were still entertainments and dances in the Hut on the Devizes road. Later, very popular barn dances were held in the barn where the grain drier is now.

Ernest Pearce who worked as a roadman keeping the ditches and drains clear, organised coach outings to Weymouth or Swanage, via Salisbury. Two or three coaches would be hired so that the young people could travel in one and stop in Salisbury for the evening, whilst the families could come straight home in the other coach. Coaches were booked every year to take people to Pewsey Carnival. Football was still popular and not only among the men. Stanton had a men's team and Jean Perry and Joyce Hale played for the Honey Street ladies' team. Ladies' football was not a soft option: Jean Perry broke her leg while playing in a scratch team in the village in Coronation year.

The 1944 Butler Education Act raised the school leaving age to 15 and free secondary education was provided for everyone. Two children went to Devizes Grammar School from Stanton School. Most pupils received their entire education in Stanton and have the usual mixed memories, but on the whole it was a happy place.

Teaching – and learning – in a small schoolroom with such a wide age range could be difficult. Fred Nash remembers the school being disrupted by the children from a large family who intimidated the younger children and reduced the headmistress to tears almost every day. The situation became so bad that an angry father took matters into his own hands. Accompanied by his grownup stepson, he marched to the school, seized the troublemakers and ducked them in the school rainwater butt. The school governors, lead by Monty Read, took action. The headmistress willingly resigned and was replaced by Ernest Evans, a recently demobbed army captain. Within a week of his arrival he had imposed discipline. Mr Evans, a strict but fair man, was headmaster of the school for many years and was very well regarded in the village.

There are other memories: of children pouring their unwanted school milk down the knot holes in the wooden floor and throwing rotten goose eggs into the school room as 'stink bombs'. The father of Miss Coggins, the infants' teacher, was a postman. He would bring the children's birthday cards to school for them to see before delivering the cards to their homes. There were school outings to the pantomime in Bristol, boat trips on the canal and even a visit to London Airport. For several seasons the school football team was unbeatable in the Vale.

With little traffic on the roads children could roam more freely than today, with opportunities for scrumping fruit and playing tricks on the neighbours. There was swimming in the canal by Englands Bridge and sliding on the ice in winter. The canal was closed to traffic in 1952 after years of neglect and disuse.

The school was closed in 1969, numbers having fallen to 14. The children under the age of 11 were transferred to Alton School. Stanton children now attend Woodborough School after Alton School was closed in its turn. The school is now the village hall. In 1987 Ann Gimson, the last infants' school teacher, gave a slideshow of the pictures she had taken of school activities and outings. It was a good evening: the village hall was packed with former pupils and their own children, thoroughly enjoying their memories.

The character of Stanton has been radically altered by the enormous changes in agriculture since the war. These are due both to mechanisation and to the ever more complex systems of control and subsidies imposed by the government, and later by the European Union. The number of men employed on the farms has steadily decreased. In 1945 there were few men in the village who were not working for the three major farmers: Mr Brice at Manor Farm, Mr King at Mill Farm (formerly Stoniford Mill) and Mr Read at Church Farm. Monty Read also had a farm in Kennet which was run by his son Jim after 1947.

When Frank Perry became the Farm Manager at Church Farm in 1953, forty-three men were working on the farm, including a farrier, blacksmith, carpenter, plumber, bricklayer and about 12 tractor drivers. Frank had started work before the war in the stables, where his father was a carter, and later drove lorries and tractors. The hours were long and the work was dirty. The horses were being replaced by the tractors which had no cabs. An army greatcoat was a favourite garment for tractor drivers; it was warm and gave some protection from the dust, but men still went home with their faces white with chalk dust. The tractors were small by modern standards and up to eight could be working in a field at any one time.

Winters were more severe than now; it was not unusual to be snowed in with falls several feet deep. People kept stocks of food sufficient to last a couple of weeks. Men worked on beyond retirement age and one man, about 75 years of age, is remembered setting off to walk one day to the dairy at Tintown through a couple of feet of snow, carrying a lantern in one hand and a shovel in the other.

When milking machines were introduced (portable ones at first) only four dairymen were required. The cows were kept indoors in winter and an extra man was needed to bring in their feed – mangolds (mangel-wurzels) and huge cabbages were grown locally. The old barns on the site of *Cherry Tree Lodge* were used for battery chickens. The sheep, which had been a prominent feature of local farming for centuries, were phased out in the early 1960s. Some small flocks, mostly of the old breeds, have been kept since as a special interest.

By 1972 twenty-five full time men were employed at Church Farm. There were 2,500 laying hens in the battery. Barley predominated in the arable, with wheat and grass. A total of seven herdsmen were employed to look after the 855 cattle in the three dairies which were at Kennet, at Stanton Dairy and in the buildings which are now the Riding Stables.

Monty Read died suddenly in 1975 whilst out riding, appropriately for such a keen horseman. He was very well respected during his 60 years in Stanton and his involvement in local government had helped secure for the village the amenities it had lacked. Jim Read took over Church Farm and in due course his sons David and Bryan entered the business.

The increasing size, cost and complexity of farm machinery meant that repairs could no longer be carried out by the blacksmith and the smithy closed, reopening later for a time to shoe horses. Smaller farms were becoming uneconomic. Mr Brice left Manor Farm and the house was occupied by the Brimacombe family, whose business was J V Strong in Devizes. At Mill Farm, Edgar and Josephine Sainsbury had taken over from Mr King and were building up a successful dairy farm. They restored the handsome late 17th-century building and in traditional fashion, had it thatched with straw which they had grown themselves.

The houses in the village were gradually sold, some to the occupiers but many to incomers with jobs outside the village. Houses have been modernised and extended and new ones built, including four small bungalows for older people in Reads Close. Gardens contained more flowers and fewer vegetables. As people acquired cars the bus service dwindled to once a week and tradesmen no longer brought supplies to sell in the village. The post office, run by Deleth Fell in her garage in Hill View after the retirement of Mr and Mrs Hampshire in 1987, closed in 1993 and there is now no shop in Stanton.

The oil and petrol business run by Charlie Carey had lost much of its custom when the electricity supply came. It was taken over by Butler Oil and became a petrol depot, until it too closed and the house called *Drake's Well* was built on the site. (*Drake's Well* is the name of the first profitable oil well discovered by Butler Oil in the USA.)

In 1963 the Rector, the Rev. Hobdey, appealed in the Wiltshire Gazette for £2,500 to save the church, which was said to be in a 'general state of decay'. Over the next few years, after a lot of fundraising and the efforts of a working party, the repairs were carried out and the gallery at the west end, 'riddled with woodworm', was removed. Since then the church has been kept in good repair and restoration work has been carried out on the mural by a specialist, again made possible by sustained fund-raising by the Parochial Church Council. Stanton is now one of the 13 parishes in the Pewsey and Swanborough Anglican Team Ministry which are all facing heavy demands for money to maintain the work of the Church of England.

When the school building became the village hall in 1970 it too was in a poor condition. In 1991 it was taken over from the Diocese on a 50-year lease and since then the Village Hall Committee has steadily raised money and obtained grants. Step by step they have transformed the hall into an attractive and comfortable meeting place.

The Parish Council was set up in 1973 and has five elected members. One of the earliest items on its agenda was the report that in the previous year, Stanton had come 62nd (third from the bottom) in the Best Kept Village Competition. Stanton has never entered since – it is a working village and has other merits.

In the 1980s and 1990s there were three milk producers in Stanton: Church Farm at its dairy located south of the canal; Colin and Mervyn Davies at Stanton Dairy with a herd of over 100 dairy cattle and Edgar Sainsbury at Mill Farm with 60-70. Following David Read's decision to move to Canada, some of the land belonging to Church Farm was sold. Bryan Read gradually took over from his father. Because of falling profit margins on milk and other agricultural products, farmers were being urged to 'diversify'. This, and the general expansion of leisure activities, has brought some innovations to the Stanton scene.

Having inherited his love of horses from his father and grandfather, in 1986 Bryan Read opened the Pewsey Vale Riding Centre at the former dairy which once housed carthorses. The sound of hooves is again a familiar one in Stanton. Paragliders can be seen on fine days floating above Milk Hill. The canal has been restored by the Kennet and Avon Canal Trust and re-opened to traffic. Now a varied collection of narrow boats moors along the towpath and the competitors in the Devizes to Westminster canoe race paddle through Stanton on Good Fridays.

In case anyone had forgotten that this is still 'Moonraker' country, in recent years the Wiltshire talent for hoodwinking credulous strangers has resulted in spectacular and beautiful crop circles appearing in the fields in Stanton and Alton Barnes. The largest so far was seen in 2001, measuring 1,000 feet across and containing 400 separate circles. The phenomenon has created a lot of interest throughout the country and abroad. Crop circle devotees from all over the world gathered at The Barge Inn every summer but now fewer circles are being produced.

In 2003 the Davies brothers and Edgar Sainsbury retired and sold their two dairy farms in the south of the parish for residential use. Church Farm is now the only working farm in Stanton. There are 356 cattle, including 200 dairy cows for which two herdsmen are responsible on a job-share basis. Winter wheat predominates, with spring barley, grass and maize for animal feed and oil seed rape for conversion into fuel. The sunflowers which can now be grown due to the warmer weather are a spectacular sight. Over 100 acres have been taken out of production under the government 'set aside' scheme. There are 163 acres of 'stewardship' land to benefit wildlife, in the form of uncultivated strips around the edges of fields and winter stubble left for nesting birds. Two generations of the Read family are working on the farm which also employs 4 people. About 20 people work at the Riding Centre.[170]

With the internet, the car and not least the Wiggly Bus which provides a flexible daily service, the village is no longer a remote place and there are some successful home-based businesses. The latest venture is the building of studio/workshops in the old barns which once were part of Manor Farm.

Stanton maintains its convivial traditions. The Millennium was celebrated with a party in the village hall, an impromptu tug-of-war down Church Walk and a big bonfire on the hill. On a sunny July day in 1999, Syd and Trish Woods invited everyone in Stanton to assemble in the garden of Manor Farm House for a group photograph to be taken. Over 100 people appear in it. There are suppers and a barbecue organised by the Village Hall Committee and the Church's summer lunch in the garden of Manor Farm House. Christmas is a busy and special season, culminating in the candle-lit midnight service in the church on Christmas Eve. Carol singing is done in the traditional way round the village. Stanton's talented musicians put on concerts of a very high standard in the church. The practical side of life is not forgotten: 'Stanton Gardeners' was formed in 2006.

In Stanton we have people whose families have lived here for over a century and incomers from diverse backgrounds who share an appreciation of the beauty of the countryside and the character of the village. We are just the latest of the many generations who have lived and worked in Stanton in the Vale of Pewsey during the past three thousand years. The story continues.

Wiltshire County Council aerial photograph of Stanton, taken on 1st January 1977

On the Devizes road, circa 1949.

Mill Farm in 1982. The waterwheel was behind the mill building on the left with the slate roof.

This picture was taken at 2.30 pm on 6th June 1949, possibly as an idea for a postcard.

Last post office in Stanton – in the garage at 2 Hillview

The church in 1807; watercolour by John Buckler who was commissioned by Sir Richard Colt Hoare to paint all the Wiltshire churches.

The church in 2007.

The mural on the chancel arch painted in 1900 by Miss Berry. It was commissioned by Mr and Mrs Tayler in memory of their late mothers.

Mr and Mrs Tayler and family in the garden at Church Farm House, c 1897 or 1898.

William Nash and Meg c 1920.

Monty Read at Church Farm House.

Playing on the frozen canal at Englands Bridge - the Gimson children c 1930.

Alton Ladies' football team with two players from Stanton: Jean Perry (centre in back row) and Joyce Hale (in front row on left).

The Sunday School in the late 1890s.

The day Stanton School closed in 1969. Monty Read in the centre with the staff and children. Staff (from left to right) May Chesterman, ?, Olive Beaven, Ann Gimson, Mrs. Cook (Headmistress).

Stanton Millennium photograph taken in Joan Brimacombe's garden at Manor Farm House in July 1999. Reproduced by permission of Syd and Trish Woods.

	Left 1	2	3	4	5	6	7	8	9	10
Back Row 7	Peter GUYETT '9, Church Road'	Robin SCHNEIDER 'Prices Cottage'	Charles OSBORNE 'The Mansion'	Steve WHITTAKER 'Forge Cottage'	Bryan READ 'Laburnam Cottage'	Rob SIMPSON '6, The Row'	Terry SMITH 'Rose Cottage'	Lionel SOMMERFIELD 'Drakes Well'	John FISHER 'Mulberry Cottage'	Steve HUMPHRIES 'Drakes Well'
Row 6	Linda GUYETT '9, Church Road'	Rachael SCHNEIDER 'Prices Cottage'	Sally OSBORNE 'The Mansion'	Carol WHITTAKER 'Forge Cottage'	Jackie READ 'Laburnam Cottage'	Colin DAVIES 'The Dairy Farm'	Janet SMITH 'Rose Cottage'	Christine GREGORY 'Folly Foot'	Charlie CALKIN 'Church Farm'	Hayley HUMPHRIES 'Drakes Well'
Row 5	Michael FELL '2, Hill View'	James TARVER '1, Hill View'	Alex WYLES 'Stanton House'	Anne WYLES 'Stanton House'	Peter WYLES 'Stanton House'	Mark FELL '2, Hill View'	Piers CORBYN 'Fowler's Cottage'	Geoff TIDBURY 'Glenville'	Brian CRITCHLOW 'Lydnards'	Edgar SAINSBURY 'Mill Farm'
Row 4	Sue LINDEMAN & Tom 'Forge Cottage'	Rob LINDEMAN 'Forge Cottage'	Mary KIRBY 'Sarsons'	Joan BRIMACOMBE 'Manor Farm'	Ray KNOWLES 'New Woodlands Cottage'	Val KNOWLES 'New Woodlands Cottage'	Marian CORBYN 'Fowler's Cottage'	Pam TIDBURY 'Glenville'	Bosy Kwan CRITCHLOW 'Lydnards'	Josephine SAINSBURY 'Mill Farm'
Row 3	XXX	Francis WALLIS 'WINFORD'	Vivien ABELS '2, Calf Lane'	Alfred ABELS '2, Calf Lane'	Derek HAMES '10, Church Road'	Diana NASH '1, Read Close'	Brian HALE '1, Coate Road'	Gwen PERRY '8, Coate Road'	Grant WAKEFIELD '1, Church Road'	Jean PERRY '7, Calf Lane'
Row 2	Hector HAPGOOD 'Chez Nous'	Nick TARVER '1, Hill View'	Lizzie WYLES 'Stanton House'	James READ 'Laburnam Cottage'	Pauline HAMES '10, Church Road'	Fred NASH '1, Read Close'	Joyce HALE '1, Coate Road'	Frank PERRY '8, Coate Road'	Jim READ 'Nutscale'	Sonny PERRY '7, Calf Lane'
Front Row 1	Richard GREGORY 'Folly Foot'	James GREGORY 'Folly Foot'	Sophie SCHNEIDER 'Prices Cottage'	Tom SCHNEIDER 'Prices Cottage'	William CALKIN 'Church Farm'	Annabel CALKIN 'Church Farm'	Emma CALKIN 'Church Farm'	Harry CALKIN 'Church Farm'	Sam READ 'Laburnam Cottage'	Thomas HUMPHRIES 'Drakes Well'

	11	12	13	14	15	16	17			
Back Row 7	Vernon FABER 'The Old Rectory'	Chris FELL '2, Hill View'	Syd WOODS 'The Beeches'	Trish WOODS 'The Beeches'	Michael FRANKTON 'Cherry Tree L...'	xxx				
Row 6	Susan FABER 'The Old Rectory'	Dell FELL '2, Hill View'	Gerald TARVER '1, Hill View'	Maurice LOVETT-TURNER 'Grey Wethers'	xxx					
Row 5	Jane ILOTT 'Rockery Nook'	William ILOTT 'Rockery Nook'	Wendy TARVER '1, Hill View'	Trisha LOVETT-TURNER 'Grey Wethers'	Gillian FRANKTON 'Cherry Tree Lodge'	xxx				
Row 4	Jacqui PERSEY & James '8, Calf Lane'	Alan PERSEY & William '8, Calf Lane'	Susan BATEY & Rannoch '3, Canal Cottages'	Andrew BATEY '3, Canal Cottages'	Rob HANNA & Lawrence '2, Church Road'	Allison HANNA & Chloe '2, Church Road'	xxx			
Row 3	Margaret BAILEY '2, The Row'	Sally BEAVEN '5, The Row'	Julie SPANSWICK & William '1, Canal Cottages'	Olive BEAVEN '3, Coats Road'	Joyce MINAY '2, Reads Close'	John TOBIN '3, Reads Close'	xxx			
Row 2	Arthur BAILEY '2, The Row'	Lionel BEAVEN '5, The Row'	Philip BAILEY '1, Canal Cottages'	Chris BEAVEN '5, The Row'	Sally-Ann BEAVEN '5, The Row'	Susannah WYLES 'Stanton House'	Alice WILLIAMSON '5, Reads Close'	xxx		
Front Row 1	Joshua HUMPHRIES 'Drakes Well'	Rebecca HUMPHRIES 'Drakes Well'	Ellie PERSEY '8, Calf Lane'	Archie OSBORNE 'The Mansion'	Isabel OSBORNE 'The Mansion'	George OSBORNE 'The Mansion'	xxx			

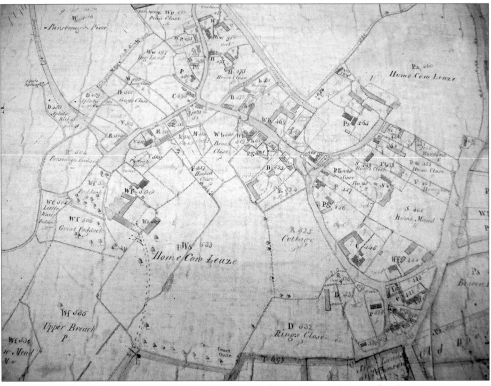

Part of Pembroke Estate map of 1784. Reproduced by permission of Wilton House.

Key to the 1784 map

Estate tenants or freeholders

B 472	Mary Buckland
C 445	Elizabeth Church
D 523	Thomas Dyke
Dw 454	Daniel Dyke
F 453	Daniel Fowle
H 473	Widow Howson
M 514	William Maslin
P 496	Elizabeth Perry
Pg 446	John Godwin
Ps 465	Isaac Simpkins
S 450	Mary Stroud
V 511	Vicarage
Wb 469	Barbara Wyndham
Wb 519	Barbara Wyndham
Wf 508	Barbara Wyndham
Wg	Thomas Walter
b 470	John Berrett
c 522	Thomas Cowdray
e 442	Richard Etwall
h 520	Samuel Hamlen
k 573	Benjamin King
r 528	Thomas Reeks
f 498	Thomas Springbatt

fg 498	John Springbatt
fs 443	Thomas Springbatt
435	Richard Powell
436	Dinah Green
437	Overseers of the Poor
438	John Gilbert
439	Mary Roberts
440	William Pope
441	John Hamlen
459	Overseers of the Poor
463	William Haynes
464	Priscella Powel
467	John Tasker
468	Stephen Tasker
478	John Alexander
479	William Hamlen
480	Thomas Roberts
530	William Swadden

Key to the 1853 map

Occupiers (not necessarily owners)

25	Richard Stevens, Henry Price
26a	Daniel Harvey
32	Wm. Bunts, Wm. Wait
33	Jas. Harvey, Wm. Price

34	Joseph Wells
35	John Crook, John Bunts
37	Sarah Maslin
38	Rbt. Perry, Rich. Alexander, Rich. Price
40	John Bristo, Wm, Bunts
41	Adam Maslin
43	John Simpkins
44	Michael Tasker
45	Vicarage - Rev. G T Ward
46	John Perry
48	Geo. Swatton, Geo. Merit
49	Parish Officers: occupied by Thos Roberts, Wm. Pierce, Thos. Bunts
53	Sub-let by Wm. Clark
55	Dinah Hailstone
57	Geo. Powell
58	Methodist chapel
59	Rosannah Francis, Ephr. Bridgman
60	Blacksmiths shop and outbuildings
61	Thomas & Charles Broomham
63	Mrs Crowther

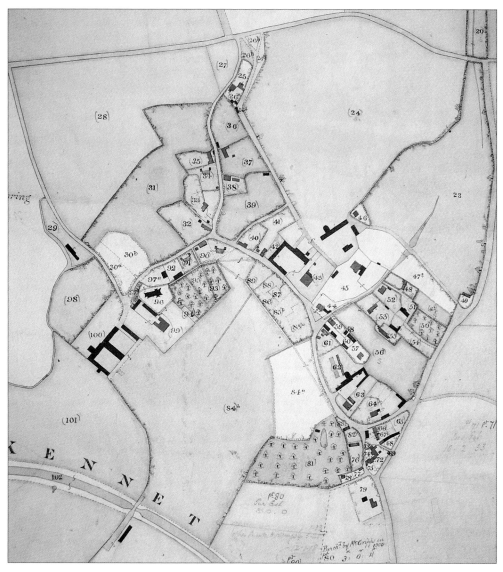

Part of Pembroke Estate map of 1853. Reproduced by permission of Wilton House.

64	Jno. Simpkins, Jno. Harvey	75	Stephen Tasker		Thos. Chandler was at the Barge Inn and James Maslin at Stanton Mill.
66	Wm. Huntley (house & shop)	76	Anthony Bristo, Jno. Stevens		
67	George Wells	77	Richard Pope		
68	John Powell, widow Alexander (house & carpenters shop)	78	Geo. Merit		The original map is in colour: houses are red and outbuildings black.
		79	William Clark		
69	John Hamlin	83	Nathaniel Popejoy		
72	Jane Fowle, Thos. Bristow, Thos. Deadman (inn, outbuildings, cottage)	90	Geo.Buckland & Hry. Hitchcock		On plots 62, 90 and 91 the houses to be built in the 1860s have been pencilled in.
		96	Church		
73	Wm. Swatton	97a	School		Those planned on plot 34 were apparently never built.
74	Charles Crook	99	Henry Hitchcock		

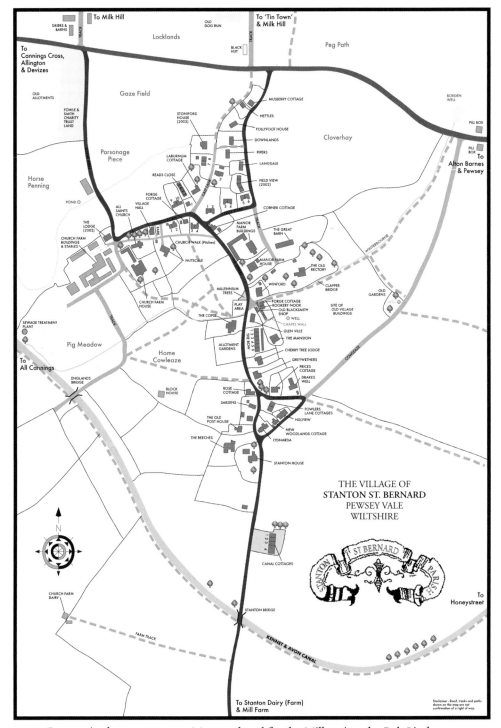

Stanton in the 21st century. Map produced for the Millennium by Rob Lindeman.

Appendices

Holders of the Manors

Holders of the estate of Stanton St Bernard

Saxon charters:.

c. 837 – 858 King Aethelwulf to Cenwold, thegn (reference in later charter – document has not survived).

905 – King Edward the Elder to Prince Ordlaf.

957 – King Eadwig to Oswulf, Bishop of Ramsbury.

960 – Grant confirmed to Bishop Oswulf by King Edgar.

1086 Held by Abbey of Wilton by this date.

1539 Abbey dissolved.

1544 Abbey estates granted to Sir William Herbert, later Earl of Pembroke..

The demesne farm

held from successive earls by leases 'on lives':.

1554 George Prater.

1567 Anthony Prater (sons of Anthony Prater surrendered lease).

1602 Thomas Baskerville. After his death held by his widow Joan.

1653 – 1751 Smith family..

c.1751 William Wyndham through his wife Barbara (née Smith). After William's death in 1762 Barbara held the estate until she died in 1786. She is shown on a map of 1773 as occupying the Manor House..

1786 Wadham Wyndham. Now occupying a new farmhouse built near the church.

Then known as Great Farm. Wadham's widow surrendered the lease to the 11th Earl in 1805.

1805 – 1871 Rack-rented (held on annual tenancy) successively to Simon Pile, Simon Hitchcock, Henry Hitchcock.In 1853 it was known as West Farm.

c.1873 James Tayler.

1915 Montague Read. Known as Church Farm.

1917 Pembroke estates sold. Montague Read purchased Church Farm.

Freehold farm

1166 Walter of Calstone held 2 hides of the Abbess of Wilton for military service.

Between **1220** and **1240** Philip of Calstone granted the land to his grandson Robert Burdon..

1240 – 1524 Burdon family.

1524 – 1567 – Farm held in two parts between Burdon and Unwin families.

1611 Death of William Unwin who had purchased the whole of the farm. Held by his widow until she died in 1618 and inherited by their two daughters.

1618 Thomas Sadler in part with John Booth (husbands of William Unwin's daughters). Thomas Sadler surrendered his interest to John Booth The farm was then known as a manor but never had tenants or courts.

1650 Thomas Booth and Reginald Bretland and their relatives.

1691 Sir Thomas Fowle (of the Charity).

1692 Susan Cope, daughter of Sir Thomas Fowle and wife of Jonathan Cope. After Susan's death in 1697, her second husband John Bartley kept the farm and in 1724 he arranged to sell it to Francis Hawes, a Director of South Sea Company which went bankrupt.

1726 The Earl of Pembroke purchased the farm from the Trustees of South Sea Company directors. Now called Little Farm, it was leased at rack rent to the Simpkins family. Manor Farm House occupied by Simpkins family from 1823.

1917 Pembroke estates sold. John Nosworthy purchased the farm, now known as Manor Farm.

The Watermills

Two mills are mentioned in Domesday Book – 1086.

.

Stanton Mill (also known as Lower Mill).

Site now Stanton Dairy.

Held by customary tenure of the Manor (Abbess of Wilton).

c. 1554 Passed to Pembroke estate, held by Hamlin family.

c.1805 Held by Simpkins family as part of Little Farm..

Not in regular use in early 19th century, water used for watermeadows..

Converted to dairy farm well before 1853.

Became known as Stanton Dairy.

Sold as part of Manor Farm in 1917 sale.

Stoniford Mill (occasionally called Upham Mill. Known as Stanton Mill after closure of the other mill) Site now Mill Farm.

1539 William Bird.

At Dissolution retained by the Crown (not included in Pembroke estate).

1546 Sir Thomas Moyle.

1551 Sir Walter Mildmay (Mill reverted to the Crown). Princess, later Queen Elizabeth.

1610 Sir Edward Ferrers and Frank Phillips.

1658 Robert Reeks held a moiety.

1667 Robert Reekes and Thomas Lavington.

1709 Thomas Lavington.

1784	Simon Pile.
1853	Still held by Pile family at this date. G W Young.

Not included in 1917 sale.

1920	Nosworthy family, owners of Manor Farm.

The holders of these mills were seldom the millers. The names of some of the millers, who were men or importance in village life, are given, with the dates at which they are known to occupy the mills.

1439	Edward Brid and John Gye.
1700	Jon Brown.
1722	James Drewet.
1747	Nathaniel Ricks.
1819	Thomas Hamlin.
1842	Michael Tasker (Upham Mill) Thomas Page (Lower Mill).
1851	Isaac Berry.
1878	James Maslen.
1881	James Maslen.
1885	Thomas Springford.
1890	William and George Springford.
1891	William Trueman.
1899	Albert Stiles.
1900	Walter J Stiles.
1912	Walter J Stiles.
1917	Albert W Perren.
1931	Albert W Perren

Money and Measurements

Money.
12 pence = 1 shilling.
20 shillings = £1 (240 pence).
21 shillings = 1 guineas.

Weight.
1 hundredweight (cwt.) = 45.36 kilos.

Length (Old maps give: furlongs and chains).

12'	1 foot		30.5 cm
3 feet	1 yard		91.5 cm
220 yards	10 chains	1 furlong	201 metres
8 furlongs	1 mile		1.6 Km

Conveniently 5 Furlongs = 1 Km

Area (Maps up to about 1970 give: acres / roods / perches).

1 acre	4 roods	160 sq perches	4840 square yards	0.4 hectare
1 hide	4 virgates	ca. 100 -120 acres		ca. 50.0 hectares
1 yardland		ca. 20 – 30 acres		ca. 8 – 12 hectares

Conveniently 2.5 Acres = 1 Hectare

Parish Registers 1568–1812

1586 Agatha died in travail and is buried with her child.

1587 John Burden buried, 'his testmonyel written' John Stratton, a travelling man, buried.

1598 14 burials recorded (average for the period 5 – 6).

1595 'A poor begging man' buried.

1609 Buried 'Ye shepherd who was found dead in ye snow'. (December 26th).

1685 Buried 'A wandering boy called William Gurgill'.

1694 Buried Robert Pike, 'killed by a wagon'.

1703 'Sarah White and Barbara Davey, sisters were buried in the same grave'.

1712 Baptised. 'Mary, base born daughter of Nathaniel Reeks and Jane his now wife' On paper pasted in and marked sent to John Shorthose (vicar 1687 – 1721) 'A Communion Salver to be delivered to the Minister of Stanton for the use of his Parish with the Charge that as soon as he meets with anyone whose Business it is to know how he came by it, he should be sure to tell him'.

1734 'A great and terrible hurricane on Wednesday 6th June about noon'.

1734-1780 Nearly every burial entry has 'buried in woolen only' (as the Act required).

1739 'A severe frost began on Christmas Eve and continued 10 weeks with great snow which melted away gently without rain and was attended by drying winds to the 11th April'.

1739 George Bezant of Alton Barnes married Mary Godwin of Stanton 'Both widdows Aged above 70 Each'.

1757 William Helps buried aged 86 or 87 after having been clerk of the parish some 60 years.

1780 15 burials recorded (4 in one grave) most occurring between February and April..

1782/1785/1791 Deaths from smallpox mentioned.

1761-1830 During these seven decades there were 154 marriages. Seventy one of the men (46%) and 113 women (73%) signed by making a mark. Infant mortality was high. Still-born or very young babies were buried under the yew tree in the churchyard..

Population

Year	Stanton St Bernard	Wiltshire	Year	Stanton St Bernard	Wiltshire
1676	120 (adults only)		1891	273	264,997
1744	247		1901	242	271,394
1801	297	185,107	1911	232	286,822
1811	296	193,828	1921	212	292,208
1821	332	222,157	1931	209	303,373
1831	319	240,156	1951	206	386,692
1841	362	258,733	1961	196	422,950
1851	349	254,221	1971	159	486,747
1861	358	249,311	1981	148	518,545
1871	371	257,177	1991	141	564,471
1881	327	258,965	2001	161	613,024

Sources:

1676 – Bishop Compton. 1744 – Rev. Thomas Smith. 1801 – 2001 – Wiltshire County Council. 1841 census includes 6 people on canal boats. 1891 census corrected (pop. given as 373 in VCH).

School Teachers and Pupils

Date	Teacher	Roll	Average Attendance
1818			
1834	William Rabbets		
1848	Charles Broomham and Mary Anne Powell		
1849	Charles Broomham and Mary Adam		
1851	Charles Broomham and Jane Tasker		
1859	Charles Broomham	30	
1881	Charles Broomham and Mary Anne Broomham	60	40
1890	John Moorhouse	50	44
1899	John Moorhouse	50	34
1903	J W Peaker and Mrs J W Peaker	70	47
1907	Mrs Blackburn	58	32
1911	Mrs Blackburn		
1920	Miss E M Rogers	45	
1923	Miss E M Rogers	57	
1927	Miss Winifred Bull	57	
1937	Mrs Payne		
	Miss Coggins		
	Mrs Huntley		
1947	Miss Rose		
1949	E Evans		
1954	Mrs Cook		
1969	Mrs Cook, Ann Gimson, May Chesterman and Olive Beaven at closure of school	14	

Surnames

	No. of entries	First	Last.
Alexander	37	1619	1803
Bayly	6	1597	1614
Buckland	44	1734	1782
Burdon	25	1568	1643
Cromwell	33	1570	1722
Fowle (Foull, Vowle, etc)	49	1584	1809
Godwin (Godwen, Godwyn)	46	1569	1793
Hamlen (Hamlin, etc)	62	1610	1792
Lavington	31	1570	1776
Lydall (Liddel, etc)	30	1574	1734
Maslen / Maslin	27	1704	1809
Naish	14	1717	1791
Pearce (Pierce)	24	1731	1807
Perry (Parry, Peary, etc)	18	1637	1811
Pile (Pyle)	5	1657	1812
Pope	27	1716	1811
Powell (Powel)	42	1630	1807
Rabbets	55	1670	1805
Reekes (Recks)	30	1619	1792
Simpkins (Simkins)	6	1777	1811
Springbatt (Springbat)	33	1658	1777
Smith	71	1596	1810
Tasker	30	1691	1802
Walter	29	1645	1800

The War Memorials

Great War 1914 – 1918.

Those who died:

Albert Bristow, 2nd November 1917.
Albert Chivers, 16th June 1915.
Herbert Crook, 29th October 1914.
Frederick Doggett, 24th April 1917.
Tom Doggett, 24th August 1918.
Richard Norris, 15th June 1915.
Archibald Pearce, 14th July 1917.
Frederick Snook, 3rd September 1916.

Another memorial given by the Simpkins family lists the same names with two additions:.

James Brown.   Reginald Kew.

Those who served are named on a separate panel:.

A H Chivers; A E G Clifford; E W J Clifford;.
R C Hams; F Hughes; E Jackman; T Lee;.
T Maslen; J Norris; G C Pearce; P J Pearce;.
J P Perrin; G Perry; T C Perry; T J Price;.
G Rutter; W Rutter; R Tayler; F W Waithman.

Second World War 1939 – 1945.

Those who died;

Frederick Price, 2nd May 1942.
Leslie Waters, 2nd March 1942.

Vicars and Rectors

1362	William Palmere	1663	Samuel Combes
	Richard Forsthulle	1665	Thomas Crapon
1385	Robert Godman	1687	John Shorthose
1391	William Huket	1721	James Wall
1393	William Couper	1728	Thomas Smith
1405	John Hereford	1760	John Harrington
1433	John Wygger	1767	John Eyre
1434	Thomas Webbe	1776	Thomas Bromley
	Robert Gerard	1812	Walter Birch
1444	John Beale	1830	George Majendie
1472	Thomas Clyff	1839	George Thompson Ward
1477	Richard Perry	1877	Henry Clark Powell
	William Thomas	1882	John Fletcher Dixon Stewart
1516	John Gold	1905	Edward Montagu Parker
1528	Nicholas Lee	1913	Francis William Topham Waithman
1531	John Spynke	1925	Sidney Lambert
1548	Michael Toppying	1932	Nathaniel Llewellyn Jenkins
	Adrian Redlegge	1946	William Henry Hobdey
1569	William Cromwell	1969	Michael Northwood
1604	Richard Stevens	1974	Team Ministry Established
1660	Samuel Baxter		

References

1 Henge – a monument of wood or stone resembling the circle of stones at Stonehenge (*Concise Oxford Dictionary*).

2 VCH Vol;. I.

3 Chandler, J. (1991) *The Vale of Pewsey*. Bradford-on-Avon. Ex Libris Press.

4 Pollard, J. & Reynolds, A. (2002) *Avebury – The Biography of a Landscape*. Stroud. Tempus.

5 Wiltshire Heritage Museum, Devizes.

6 Ibid.

7 Malone, C. (1989) *Avebury*. London. English Heritage.

8 Pollard, J. & Reynolds, A. (2002) *Avebury – The Biography of a Landscape*. Stroud. Tempus.

9 Ibid.

10 Piggott, S. (1993) 'John Thurnam (1810-1873) and British Prehistory'. WAM Vol.86.

11 now said to be in the British Museum.

12 Malone, C. (1989) *Avebury*. London. English Heritage.

13 The sarsens occur naturally in Wiltshire, and were once scattered over the fields to the great inconvenience of farmers. A field of sarsens can be seen in Lockeridge village.

14 Ordnance Survey map 1887.

15 Information from Mr J Read.

16 Wiltshire Heritage Museum, Devizes.

17 Ibid.

18 Ibid.

19 WAM Vol. 64, p 114. and catalogue of Bronze Age metalwork in Salisbury Museum. The palstaves are from a private collection, donated to Salisbury Museum before 1864 and are in poor condition.

20 Wiltshire Heritage Museum, Devizes.

21 Many of these finds can be seen in the Wiltshire Heritage Museum, Devizes.

22 By Mr Frederick Nash of Stanton.

23 Diary of the dig posted on Kennet District Council website, 6th – 19th September 2004, and lecture subsequently given by Professor John Barrett in Stanton St Bernard Village Hall.

24 Robinson, P H. (1993) 'Iron Age coins from Cunetio and Mildenhall'. WAM Vol. 86.

25 Potter, T W, & Johns, C. (1992) Roman Britain. London. British Museum.

26 Ibid. Image of the carving is in the Corinium Museum, Cirencester.

27 Pollard, J & Reynolds, A. (2002) Avebury – The Biography of a Landscape. Stroud. Tempus.

28 Potter, T W & Johns, C. (1992) Roman Britain. London. British Museum.

29 The 'Stanchester Hoard' in Wiltshire Heritage Museum.

30 'Blacknall Field' – Dr Bruce Eagles.

31 The Anglo-Saxon Chronicle Editor: Christopher Pick (1982) London. Heineman.

32 Bede (AD731) History of the English Church and People.

33 Translation: F E Harmer from Stanton and its People by Naomi Corbyn.

34 Sawyer, P.H. (1968) Anglo-Saxon Charters. London. Royal Historical Society. Charter for part of Alton Barnes AD 825.

35 Reynolds, A. (1999) Later Anglo-Saxon England. Stroud. Tempus. The date is given as 903 in Anglo-Saxon Charters by P Sawyer.

36 Reynolds. A. ('From Pagus to Parish,' in The Avebury Landscape ed. Brown, Field and McOmish.

37 Sawyer, P.H. (1968) Anglo-Saxon Charters (AD900 Ordlaf with Bishop of Winchester, AD901 Ordlaf with church in Malmesbury.).

38 Ibid.

39 Translation reproduced by kind permission of Dr Andrew Reynolds Later Anglo-Saxon England.

40 Reynolds, A. (1999) Later Anglo-Saxon England. Stroud. Tempus.

41 See The Vale of Pewsey by John Chandler for a discussion of the Hundreds in the Vale. It is suggested that by the time of the Domesday survey Swanborough was a 'double Hundred'.

42 Ordnance Survey grid reference SU130600.

43 Fowler, P. (2001) paper 'Wansdyke in the Woods'. From Ellis, P. ed. (2001) Roman Wiltshire and after. Devizes. WANHS.

44 Reynolds, A. (1999) Later Anglo-Saxon England. Stroud. Tempus.

45 Reynolds, A. (1999) Later Anglo-Saxon England. Stroud. Tempus. This is the plan of Goltho, Lincolnshire, which seems to fit the later development of Stanton. An alternative plan is that of Anglo-Saxon Avebury, where the houses were grouped together within a boundary fence.

46 Fowler, P. & Blackwell, I. (1998) An English Countryside Explored – The land of Lettice Sweetapple. Stroud. Tempus.

47 Wiltshire Heritage Museum, Devizes.

48 Haywood, J. (1995) The Penguin Historical Atlas of the Vikings. London. Penguin.

49 Ibid.

50 Anglo-Saxon Chronicle – royal edict of the year 1007.

51 Wood, M. (1999) Domesday. London. BBC Worldwide Ltd.

52 Wiltshire Heritage Museum, Devizes.

53 Wiltshire Heritage Museum, Devizes.

54 Houses of Benedictine Nuns British History Online – VCH.

55 Anglo-Saxon Chronicle 'Domesday' is from the old English 'dom' meaning an assessment.

56 Morris, J. ed. (1979) Domesday Book. Chichester. Phillimore.

57 A league was a measurement of distance for travelling – usually reckoned at 3 miles.

58 Ibid.

59 A hide was the area of land reckoned necessary to support an extended family. Its size varied according to the fertility of the land.

60 Survey of the lands of the Earl of Pembroke, 1563 printed in 1909 for the Roxburghe Club.

61 Crown Pleas of Wiltshire Eyre 1249. Wiltshire Record Society, Vol. 16.

62 C. Dyer Making a living in the Middle Ages Penguin, London 2003.

63 Wiltshire Tax List of 1332 Wiltshire Record Society

Vol. 45.

64 The Ordinance of Labourers (1349), the Statute of Labourers (1349), the Statue of Cambridge (1388).

65 C. Dyer *Making a living in the Middle Ages* Penguin, London 2003.

66 WAM (Corbyn).

67 C Dyer *Making a living in the Middle Ages* Penguin, London 2003.

68 *Victoria County History.*

69 N. Corbyn (1986) *Stanton and its people.*

70 *All Saints Church, Stanton St Bernard .*

71 N. Corbyn (1986) *Stanton and its people.*

72 *Wiltshire Notes and Cuttings* Wiltshire Heritage Library. The original source has not been traced.

73 pyx – a vessel in which the consecrated bread for the mass is kept.

74 N. Corbyn (1986) *Stanton and its people* – passage found in 'Wiltshire Tracts', Wiltshire Heritage Library.

75 The survey was published in 1909 by the Earl of Pembroke for the Roxburghe Club.

76 Baynton, Burdon, Dyer, Goodwyn, Hamlen, Hichcok, Hochens, Knyght, Lavington, Ledall, Moyle, Plotte, Prater, Rogers, Smithe, Stronge, Unyon, Vowle and Wyett.

77 An indenture was a contract between two parties in which each kept half the document, cut along an indented line.

78 These tenants held their land by copy of the entry in the manor court roll. The copyholders were the successors of the medieval villains – 16 copyholders in Stanton in 1567 and 16 villeins mentioned in Domesday in 1086.

79 *Extracts from Quarter Sessions Great Rolls* – Records of the county of Wiltshire – Edited by B H Cunnington 1932. Wiltshire Heritage Library.

80 There is no record of his baptism in the Parish Register.

81 Newbury Town website.

82 Manuscript found in the church safe in Stanton.

83 *Wiltshire Tracts*, Wiltshire Heritage Library.

84 yardland – originally related to the area of land which could be worked by a team of oxen. Later it was reckoned at a quarter of a hide and could vary between 20 and 50 statute acres, depending on the type of land.

85 *Wiltshire Glebe Terriers 1588-1827* Ed. Steve Hobbs, Wiltshire Record Society, Vol. 56, 2003.

86 1660 according to the modern calendar. Before 1752 the year ended on 25th March, not 1st January.

87 N. Corbyn (1986) *Stanton and its people.*

88 *Will of Thomas Fowle 1692* The National Archives, Public Record Office, catalogue ref: Prob/11/413.

89 *Will of Isaac Smith 1720* The National Archives, Public Record Office, catalogue ref: Prob/11/574.

90 3 acres, 3 rods and 25 perches.

91 *Manorial Court Book* Earl of Pembroke WRO Ref: 2057/M70.

92 *Survey of Stanton St Bernard 1785* Earl of Pembroke WRO Ref: 2057/S72.

93 *Wiltshire Coroner's Bills 1752-96* Ed. R F Hunnisett, Wiltshire Record Society, Vol.36, 1981.

94 *Lurgashall Mill* Weald & Downland Open Air Museum.

95 A mill for grinding corn where the water is channelled to the upper part of the waterwheel.

96 *Wiltshire Returns of Bishop's Visitation Queries 1783* Ed. M Ransome, Wiltshire Record Society, Vol.27, 1972.

97 Jeremy, J.D. 'A local crisis between Establishment and Nonconformity – The Salisbury Village Preaching controversy 1798-99', WAM, Vol. 61.

98 *Wiltshire Dissenters' Meeting House Certificates 1689-1852*, Wiltshire Record Society, Vol. 40, 1985.

99 Kenneth Clew *The Kennet & Avon Canal* David & Charles, Newton Abbot 1985

100 Morris Marples *White Horses and other Hill Figures* 1981 Alan Sutton Publishing Ltd., Gloucester.

101 *Stanton Parish Book*, Wiltshire & Swindon Record Office, Ref: 2303/12.

102 D Anderson 'Noyfull Fowles and Vermyn: Parish Payments for Killing Wildlife in Wiltshire, 1533 – 1863' WAM ,Vol 98 2005.

103 E J Hobsbawn & G Rudé *Captain Swing* 1969 Lawrence & Wishart.

104 *Salisbury & Wiltshire Journal* 10th January 1831.

105 *Wiltshire Notes and Queries* and The Patent Office.

106 *Stanton Parish Book* Wiltshire & Swindon Record Office, ref: 2303/5.

107 As both William Fowle and Isaac Smith died in London, their Wills are in the National Archive in London.

108 *Devizes & Wiltshire Gazette* 13th March 1834.

109 Wiltshire & Swindon Record Office ref: 867/1.

110 W. Berry, *Robbins, Lane & Pinneger — a canal based enterprise* 2004 The Butty, K & A Trust and D Harris *Honey Street Wharf* 2006 The Butty, K & A Trust.

111 C & H Hackford *The Kennet & Avon Canal* 2001 Tempus , Stroud.

112 *Victoria County History* Vol X.

113 *Pollbooks* for 1819 and 1842 elections, Wiltshire Heritage Library.

114 *Church Faculty* 1859 Wiltshire & Swindon Record Office D1/61/11/9.

115 *Wilton Memoranda* Wiltshire & Swindon Record Office ref: 2057/E2/4.

116 Wiltshire Heritage Library.

117 *Papers in case of Deadman v Fidler* Wiltshire & Swindon Record Office ref 1225/181.

118 From Mr J Read.

119 Charity Commission report of 27th August 1890 .

120 Records of the Fowle & Smith Charity.

121 *Early motor vehicle registration in Wiltshire* ed Ian Hicks Wiltshire Record Society Vol 58.

122 Holmes, R *Tommy* Harper Collins, London 2004.

123 N Wilts Parish Magazine.

124 early form of slide projector, using glass slides and powered by a candle or oil lamp.

125 Mr J Read *Memoirs*.

126 Ibid.

127 Slocombe I, 'Agriculture in Wiltshire in the First World War', WAM, Vol 95.

128 Ibid.

129 Sale catalogue Wiltshire Heritage Library.

130 Albert Bristow served with the Hampshire Regiment and was buried in Gaza.

131 Fred Nash.

132 Stanton Diary: WRO ref 2303/12.

133 Vestry Minutes: WRO ref 2303/16.

134 N Wilts Parish Magazine.

135 Ibid.

136 Ibid.

137 Ibid.

138 Ibid.

139 Ibid.

140 N. Corbyn (1986) *Stanton and its people*.

141 Memoir – Mr J Read.

142 Ibid.

143 Mr F Nash.

144 Mr J Read.

145 Mr Fred Nash.

146 Memoir – Mr J Read.

147 Memoir – Mr J Read.

148 N. Corbyn (1986) *Stanton and its people*.

149 Berryman D (2002) *Wiltshire Airfields in the Second World War*. Countryside Books, Newbury.

150 N Wilts Parish Magazine.

151 Ibid.

152 Joyce Hale.

153 Vera Ostergaard.

154 Devizes Local History Group *How Devizes won the War* .

155 Memoir – J Read.

156 *N. Wilts Parish Magazine* – Edward Hudson, Leslie Waters, Bert Hams, Willie Head, Bert Bailey.

157 Joyce Hale.

158 information from Ann Gimson and Vera Ostergaard.

159 Gardiner, J. (2004) *Wartime Britain 1939-1945*. London. Headline Book Publishing.

160 N. Corbyn (1986) *Stanton and its people*.

161 Ashworth, C. (1990) *Action Stations: military airfields of the South-West*. Wellingborough: Patrick Stephens Ltd.

162 Berryman, D. (2002) *Wiltshire Airfields in the Second World War*. Newbury: Countryside Books.

163 Jim Read.

164 Vera Ostergaard.

165 *N. Wilts Parish Magazine*.

166 N. Corbyn (1986) *Stanton and its people*.

167 information from Vera Ostergaard.

168 N. Corbyn (1986) *Stanton and its people.*

169 Stanton Register of Services 1940-51:WRO ref 2303/2.

170 Information on farming was kindly provided by Frank Perry, Sonny and Jean Perry, Bryan and Jacky Read, Edgar and Josephine Sainsbury.

Other Sources

Victoria County History of the Counties of England,Wiltshire, Vols. 1, 4 and 10.

North Wilts. Parish Magazines, late 19th – mid 20th centuries. Wiltshire Heritage Library, Devizes

Directories: Kellys and Gilmans – various dates

Bettey J. H. *Rural Life in Wessex* 1500-1900 Gloucester. Alan Sutton Publishing. 1987

Bettey J.H. 'Some Evidence for Livestock Traffic in Wiltshire during the Seventeenth Century' *WAM* Vol.81, 1987

Cobbett W. *Rural Rides.* London. Penguin Books. 1985

Cowan. M. *Wiltshire Water Meadows.* Salisbury. The Hobnob Press. 2005

Crawford T. S. *Wiltshire and the Great War.* Reading. DPF Publishing 1999

Crittall. E. (Ed) *The Justicing Notebook of William Hunt 1744-1749.* Wiltshire Record Society Vol. 37, 1982

Dyer C. *Everyday Life in Medieval England.* London. Hambledon and London. 1994

Green M. *A Landscape Revealed. 10,000 years on a Chalkland Farm.* Stroud. Tempus. 2000

Hackford C. & H. *The Kennet & Avon Canal.* Stroud. Tempus Publishing Limited. 2001

Hall A. *Land Girl.* Bradford-on-Avon. Ex Libris Press. 1993

Hicks. I. *Early Motor Vehicle Registration in Wiltshire 1903-14.* Wiltshire Record Society Vol. 59, 2006

Kerridge E. (Ed) *Surveys of the Manors of Philip, Earl of Pembroke and Montgomery 1631-32.* Wiltshire Record Society Vol. 9, 1953

Lacey R. & Danziger D. *The Year 1000.* Boston. Little, Brown and Company. 1999

Mitchell D.M. 'Dressing plate by the "unknown" London silversmith "W.F."' *The Burlington Magazine.* Vol. 135. London. June 1993.

Mitchell D.M. *Mr Fowle Pray Pay the Washerwoman – the trade of a London Goldsmith-Banker, 1660-1692.* Website

Moore C. N. & Rowlands M. *Bronze Age Metalwork in Salisbury Museum.* Salisbury. Salisbury and South Wiltshire Museum Occasional Publication 1972

Moore C.N. 'Notes – Five unpublished bronze implements from Wiltshire' *WAM* Vol.64, 1969

Rickard R. L. (Ed) *Progress notes of Warden Woodward for the Wiltshire Estates of New College, Oxford 1659-1675.* Wiltshire Record Society Vol.13, 1957

Salway P. & Blair J. *Oxford History of Britain - Roman and Anglo-Saxon Britain.* Oxford. Oxford University Press. 1984

Timperley H.W. *The Vale of Pewsey.* Hale. 1954

Willoughby R.W.H. 'Water-mills in West Wiltshire' *WAM* Vol.64, 1964

Wroughton J. *An Unhappy Civil War.* Bath. The Lansdown Press. 1999

Wiltshire Tax List of 1332. Wiltshire Record Society Vol.45

WAM = The Wiltshire Archaeological and Natural History Magazine

WRO = Wiltshire & Swindon Record Office

Index

This is principally an index of names and places, with selected subjects. Names of houses and buildings in Stanton are printed in *italics*. The millennium photograph (pp. 136-7), place-names on maps, and the appendices have not been indexed.